on
the Orient

Published by Hesperus Press Limited
28 Mortimer Street, London W1W 7RD
www.hesperuspress.com

Selection taken from collected journalism entitled 'From Sea to Sea',
published between 1887–89
First published by Hesperus Press Limited, 2014

Designed and typeset by Fraser Muggeridge studio
Printed in Great Britain CPI Group (UK) Ltd, Croydon, CR0 4YY

ISBN: 978-1-84391-624-6

All rights reserved. This book is sold subject to the condition that it shall
not be resold, lent, hired out or otherwise circulated without the express
prior consent of the publisher.

Kipling
on
the Orient

'on'

India

Of the beginning of things. Of the Taj and the Globetrotter. The young man from Manchester and certain moral reflections.

Except for those who, under compulsion of a sick certificate, are flying Bombaywards, it is good for every man to see some little of the great Indian Empire and the strange folk who move about it. It is good to escape for a time from the House of Rimmon – be it office or cutchery – and to go abroad under no more exacting master than personal inclination, and with no more definite plan of travel than has the horse, escaped from pasture, free upon the countryside. The first result of such freedom is extreme bewilderment, and the second reduces the freed to a state of mind which, for his sins, must be the normal portion of the Globetrotter – the man who 'does' kingdoms in days and writes books upon them in weeks. And this desperate facility is not as strange as it seems. By the time that an Englishman has come by sea and rail *via* America, Japan, Singapore, and Ceylon, to India, he can – these eyes have seen him do so – master in five minutes the intricacies of the *Indian Bradshaw*, and tell an old resident exactly how and where the trains run. Can we wonder that the intoxication of success in hasty assimilation should make him overbold, and that he should try to grasp – but a full account of the insolent Globetrotter must be reserved. He is worthy of a book. Given absolute freedom for a month, the mind, as I have said, fails to take in the situation and, after much debate, contents itself with following in old and well-beaten ways – paths that we in India have no time to tread, but must leave to the country cousin who wears his *pagri* tail-fashion down his back, and says 'cabman' to the driver of the *ticca-ghari*.

Now, Jeypore from the Anglo-Indian point of view is a station on the Rajputana-Malwa line, on the way to Bombay, where half an hour is allowed for dinner, and where there ought to be more protection from the sun than at present exists. Some few, more learned than the rest, know that garnets come from Jeypore, and here the limits of our wisdom are set. We do not, to quote the Calcutta shopkeeper, come out 'for the good of our 'ealth', and what touring we accomplish is for the most part off the line of rail.

For these reasons, and because he wished to study our winter birds of passage, one of the few thousand Englishmen in India on a date and in a place which have no concern with the story, sacrificed all his self-respect and became – at enormous personal inconvenience – a Globetrotter going to Jeypore, and leaving behind him for a little while all that old and well-known life in which Commissioners and Deputy-Commissioners, Governors and Lieutenant-Governors, Aides-de-camp, Colonels and their wives, Majors, Captains, and Subalterns after their kind move and rule and govern and squabble and fight and sell each other's horses and tell wicked stories of their neighbours. But before he had fully settled into his part or accustomed himself to saying, 'Please take out this luggage', to the coolies at the stations, he saw from the train the Taj wrapped in the mists of the morning.

There is a story of a Frenchman who feared not God, nor regarded man, sailing to Egypt for the express purpose of scoffing at the Pyramids and – though this is hard to believe – at the great Napoleon who had warred under their shadow. It is on record that that blasphemous Gaul came to the Great Pyramid and wept through mingled reverence and contrition; for he sprang from an emotional race. To understand his feelings it is necessary to have read a great deal too much about the Taj, its design and proportions; to have seen execrable pictures of it at the Simla Fine Arts Exhibition, to have had its praises sung by superior and travelled friends till the brain loathed the repetition of the word; and then, sulky with want of sleep, heavy-eyed, unwashed, and chilled, to come upon it suddenly. Under these circumstances everything, you will concede, is in favour of a cold, critical, and not too impartial verdict. As the Englishman leaned out of the carriage he saw first an opal-tinted cloud on the horizon, and, later, certain towers. The mists lay on the ground, so that the splendour seemed to be floating free of the earth; and the mists rose in the background, so that at no time could everything be seen clearly. Then as the train sped forward, and the mists shifted, and the sun shone upon the mists, the Taj took a hundred new shapes, each perfect and each beyond description. It was the Ivory Gate through which all good dreams come; it was the realization of 'the gleaming halls of dawn' that Tennyson sings of; it was veritably the 'aspiration fixed', the 'sigh made stone' of a lesser poet; and, over and above concrete comparisons, it seemed the embodiment of all things pure, all things holy, and all things unhappy. That was the mystery of the building! It may be that the mists wrought the witchery, and that the Taj seen in the dry sunlight is only, as guidebooks say, a noble structure. The Englishman could not tell, and has made a vow that he will never go nearer the spot, for fear of breaking the charm of the unearthly pavilions.

It may be, too, that each must view the Taj for himself with his own eyes, working out his own interpretation of the sight. It is certain that no man can in cold blood and colder ink set down his impressions if he has been in the least moved.

To the one who watched and wondered that November morning the thing seemed full of sorrow – the sorrow of the man who built it for the woman he loved, and the sorrow of the workmen who died in the building – used up like cattle. And in the face of this sorrow the Taj flushed in the sunlight and was beautiful, after the beauty of a woman who has done no wrong.

Here the train ran in under the walls of Agra Fort, and another train – of thought incoherent as that written above – came to an end. Let those who scoff at overmuch enthusiasm look at the Taj and thenceforward be dumb. It is well on the threshold of a journey to be taught reverence and awe.

But there is no reverence in the Globetrotter: he is brazen. A Young Man from Manchester was travelling to Bombay in order – how the words hurt! – to be home by Christmas. He had come through America, New Zealand, and Australia, and finding that he had ten days to spare at Bombay, conceived the modest idea of 'doing India'. 'I don't say that I've done it all; but you may say that I've seen a good deal.' Then he explained that he had been 'much pleased' at Agra; 'much pleased' at Delhi; and, last profanation, 'very much pleased' at the Taj. Indeed, he seemed to be going through life just then 'much pleased' at everything. With rare and sparkling originality he remarked that India was a 'big place', and that there were many things to buy. Verily, this Young Man must have been a delight to the Delhi boxwallahs. He had purchased shawls and embroidery 'to the tune of' a certain number of rupees duly set forth, and he had purchased jewellery to another tune. These were gifts for friends at home, and he considered them 'very Eastern'. If silver filigree work modelled on Palais Royal patterns, or aniline blue scarves be Eastern, he had succeeded in his heart's desire. For some inscrutable end it had been decreed that man shall take a delight in making his fellow man miserable. The Englishman began to point out gravely the probable extent to which the Young Man from Manchester had been swindled, and the Young Man said: 'By Jove! You don't say so? I hate being done. If there's anything I hate, it's being done!'

He had been so happy in the thought of 'getting home by Christmas', and so charmingly communicative as to the members of his family for whom such and such gifts were intended, that the Englishman cut short the record of fraud and soothed him by saying that he had not been so very badly 'done', after all. This consideration was misplaced, for, his peace of mind restored, the Young Man from Manchester looked out of the window and, waving his hand over the Empire generally, said: 'I say. Look here. All those wells are wrong, you know!' The wells were on the wheel and inclined plane system; but he objected to the incline, and said that it would be much better for the bullocks if they walked on level ground. Then light dawned upon him, and he said: 'I suppose it's to exercise all their muscles. Y'know a canal horse is no use after he has been on the towpath for some time. He can't walk anywhere but on the flat, y'know, and I suppose it's just the same with bullocks.' The spurs of the Aravalis, under which the train was running, had evidently suggested this brilliant idea which passed uncontradicted, for the Englishman was looking out of the window.

If one were bold enough to generalise after the manner of Globetrotters, it would be easy to build up a theory on the well incident to account for the apparent insanity of some of our cold weather visitors. Even the Young Man from Manchester could evolve a complete idea for the training of well-bullocks in the East at thirty seconds' notice. How much the more could a cultivated observer from, let us say, an English constituency, blunder and pervert and mangle? We in this country have no time to work out the notion, which is worthy of the consideration of some leisurely Teuton intellect.

Envy may have prompted a too bitter judgement of the Young Man from Manchester; for, as the train bore him from Jeypore to Ahmedabad, happy in his 'getting home by Christmas', pleased as a child with his Delhi atrocities, pink-cheeked, whiskered, and superbly self-confident, the Englishman whose home for the time was a dark bungaloathsome hotel, watched his departure regretfully; for he knew exactly to what sort of genial, cheery British household, rich in untravelled kin, that Young Man was speeding. It is pleasant to play at Globetrotting; but to enter fully into the spirit of the piece, one must also be 'going home for Christmas'.

The temple of Mahadeo and the manners of such as see India. The man by the water-troughs and his knowledge. The voice of the city and what it said. Personalities and the hospital. The house beautiful of Jeypore and its builders.

From the cotton press the Englishman wandered through the wide streets till he came into an Hindu temple – rich in marble stone and inlay, and a deep and tranquil silence, close to the Public Library of the State. The brazen bull was hung with flowers, and men were burning the evening incense before Mahadeo; while those who had prayed their prayer beat upon the bells hanging from the roof and passed out, secure in the knowledge that the God had heard them. If there be much religion, there is little reverence, as Westerns understand the term, at the services of the Gods of the East. A tiny little maiden, child of a monstrously ugly, wall-eyed priest, staggered across the marble pavement to the shrine and threw, with a gust of childish laughter, the blossoms she was carrying into the lap of the Great Mahadeo himself. Then she made as though she would leap up to the bell and ran away, still laughing, into the shadow of the cells behind the shrine, while her father explained that she was but a baby and that Mahadeo would take no notice. The temple, he said, was specially favoured by the Maharaja, and drew from lands an income of twenty thousand rupees a year. Thakoors and great men also gave gifts out of their benevolence; and there was nothing in the wide world to prevent an Englishman from following their example.

By this time – for Amber and the cotton press had filled the hours – night was falling, and the priests unhooked the swinging jets and began to light up the impassive face of Mahadeo with gas. They used Swedish matches!

Full night brought the hotel and its curiously composed human menagerie.

There is, if a workaday world will believe, a society entirely outside, and unconnected with, that of the station – a planet within a planet, where nobody knows anything about the Collector's wife, the Colonel's dinner party, or what was really the matter with the Engineer. It is a curious, an insatiably curious, thing, and its literature is Newman's *Bradshaw*. Wandering 'old arms-sellers' and others live upon it, and so do the garnetmen and the makers of ancient Rajput shields. The world of the innocents abroad is a touching and unsophisticated place, and its very atmosphere urges the Anglo-Indian unconsciously to an extravagant mendacity. Can you wonder, then, that a guide of long-standing should in time grow to be an accomplished liar?

Into this world sometimes breaks the Anglo-Indian returned from leave, or a fugitive to the sea, and his presence is like that of a well-known landmark in the desert. The old arms-seller knows and avoids him, and he is detested by the jobber of gharis who calls every one 'my lord' in English, and panders to the 'glaring race anomaly' by saying that every carriage not under his control is 'rotten, my lord, having been used by natives'. One of the privileges of playing at tourist is the brevet – rank of 'Lord'.

There are many, and some very curious, methods of seeing India. One of these is buying English translations of the more Zolaistic of Zola's novels and reading them from breakfast to dinnertime in the veranda. Yet another, even simpler, is American in its conception. Take a Newman's *Bradshaw* and a blue pencil, and race up and down the length of the Empire, ticking off the names of the stations 'done'. To do this thoroughly, keep strictly to the railway buildings and form your conclusions through the carriage windows. These eyes have seen both ways of working in full blast; and, on the whole, the first is the most commendable.

Let us consider now with due reverence the modern side of Jeypore. It is difficult to write of a nickel-plated civilisation set down under the immemorial Aravallis in the first state of Rajputana. The red-grey hills seem to laugh at it, and the ever-shifting sand dunes under the hills take no account of it, for they advance upon the bases of the monogrammed, coronet-crowned lamp posts, and fill up the points of the natty tramways near the waterworks, which are the outposts of the civilisation of Jeypore.

Escape from the city by the Railway Station till you meet the cactus and the mudbank and the Maharaja's cotton press. Pass between a tramway and a trough for wayfaring camels till your foot sinks ankle-deep in soft sand, and you come upon what seems to be the fringe of illimitable desert – mound upon mound of tussocks overgrown with plumed grass where the parrots sit and swing. Here, if you have kept to the road, you shall find a dam faced with stone, a great tank, and pumping machinery fine as the heart of a municipal engineer can desire – pure water, sound pipes, and well-kept engines. If you belong to what is sarcastically styled an 'able and intelligent municipality' under the British Rule, go down to the level of the tank, scoop up the water in your hands and drink, thinking meanwhile of the defects of the town whence you came. The experience will be a profitable one. There are statistics in connection with the waterworks figures relating to 'three throw plungers', delivery and supply, which should be known to the professional reader. They would not interest the unprofessional who would learn his lesson among the thronged standpipes of the city.

While the Englishman was preparing in his mind a scathing rebuke for an erring municipality that he knew of, a camel swung across the sands, its driver's jaw and brow bound mummy-fashion to guard against the dust. The man was evidently a stranger to the place, for he pulled up and asked the Englishman where the drinking troughs were. He was a gentleman and bore very patiently with the Englishman's absurd ignorance of his dialect. He had come from some village, with an unpronounceable name, thirty *kos* away, to see his brother's son, who was sick in the big hospital. While the camel was drinking the man talked, lying back along his mount. He knew nothing of Jeypore, except the names of certain Englishmen in it, the men who, he said, had made the waterworks and built the hospital for his brother's son's comfort.

And this is the curious feature of Jeypore; though happily the city is not unique in its peculiarity. When the late Maharaja ascended the throne, more than fifty years ago, it was his royal will and pleasure that Jeypore should advance. Whether he was prompted by love for his subjects, desire for praise, or the magnificent vanity with which Jey Singh must have been so largely dowered, are questions that concern nobody. In the latter years of his reign, he was supplied with Englishmen who made the state their fatherland, and identified themselves with its progress as only Englishmen can. Behind them stood the Maharaja ready to spend money with a lavishness that no Supreme Government would dream of; and it would not be too much to say that they together made the state what it is. When Ram Singh died, Madho Singh, his successor, a conservative Hindu, forbore to interfere in any way with the work that was going forward. It is said in the city that he does not overburden himself with the cares of State, the driving power being mainly in the hands of a Bengali, who has everything but the name of Minister. Nor do the Englishmen, it is said in the city, mix themselves with the business of government; their business being wholly executive.

They can, according to the voice of the city, do what they please, and the voice of the city – not in the main roads, but in the little side alleys where the stall-less bull blocks the path – attests how well their pleasure has suited the pleasure of the people. In truth, to men of action few things could be more delightful than having a state of fifteen thousand square miles placed at their disposal, as it were, to leave their mark on. Unfortunately for the vagrant traveller, those who work hard for practical ends prefer not to talk about their doings, and he must, therefore, pick up what information he can at secondhand or in the city. The men at the standpipes explain that the Maharaja Sahib's father gave the order for the waterworks and that Yakub (Jacob) Sahib made them – not only in the city, but out away in the district. 'Did the people grow more crops thereby?' 'Of course they did. Were canals made only to wash in?' 'How much more crops?' 'Who knows? The Sahib had better go and ask some official.' Increased irrigation means increase of revenue for the State somewhere, but the man who brought about the increase does not say so.

After a few days of amateur Globetrotting, a shamelessness great as that of the other loafer – the red-nosed man who hangs about one garden and is always on the eve of starting for Calcutta – possesses the masquerader; so that he feels equal to asking a Resident for a parcel-gilt howdah, or dropping into dinner with a Lieutenant-Governor. No man has a right to keep anything back from a Globetrotter, who is a mild, temperate, gentlemanly, and unobtrusive seeker after truth. Therefore he who, without a word of enlightenment, sends the visitor into a city which he himself has beautified and adorned and made clean and wholesome, deserves unsparing exposure. And the city may be trusted to betray him. The *malli* in the Ram Newas Gardens – gardens which are finer than any in India and fit to rank with the best in Paris – says that the Maharaja gave the order and Yakub Sahib made the gardens. He also says that the hospital just outside the gardens was built by Yakub Sahib, and if the Sahib will go to the centre of the gardens, he will find another big building, a museum by the same hand.

But the Englishman went first to the hospital, and found the outpatients beginning to arrive. A hospital cannot tell lies about its own progress as a municipality can. Sick folk either come or lie in their own villages. In the case of the Mayo Hospital, they came, and the operation book showed that they had been in the habit of coming. Doctors at issue with provincial and local administrations, Civil Surgeons who cannot get their indents complied with, ground down and mutinous practitioners all India over, would do well to visit the Mayo Hospital, Jeypore. They might, in the exceeding bitterness of their envy, be able to point out some defects in its supplies, or its beds, or its splints, or in the absolute isolation of the women's quarters from the men's.

From the hospital the Englishman went to the museum in the centre of the gardens, and was eaten up by it, for museums appealed to him. The casing of the jewel was in the first place superb – a wonder of carven white stone of the Indo-Saracenic style. It stood on a stone plinth, and was rich in stone tracery, green marble columns from Ajmer, red marble, white marble colonnades, courts with fountains, richly carved wooden doors, frescoes, inlay, and colour. The ornamentation of the tombs of Delhi, the palaces of Agra, and the walls of Amber have been laid under contribution to supply the designs in bracket, arch, and soffit; and stonemasons from the Jeypore School of Art have woven into the work the best that their hands could produce. The building in essence if not in the fact of today, is the work of Freemasons. The men were allowed a certain scope in their choice of detail and the result – but it should be seen to be understood, as it stands in those Imperial Gardens. And, observe, the man who had designed it, who had superintended its erection, had said no word to indicate that there were such a thing in the place, or that every foot of it, from the domes of the roof to the cool green chunam dadoes and the carving of the rims of the fountains in the courtyard, was worth studying! Round the arches of the great centre court are written in Sanskrit and Hindi, texts from the great Hindu writers of old, bearing on the beauty of wisdom and the sanctity of true knowledge.

In the central corridor are six great frescoes, each about nine feet by five, copies of illustrations in the Royal Folio of the *Razmnameh*, the *Mahabharata*, which Abkar caused to be done by the best artists of his day. The original is in the museum, and he who can steal it will find a purchaser at any price up to fifty thousand pounds.

Of the sordidness of the supreme government on the revenue side; and of the palace of Jeypore. A great king's pleasure house, and the work of the servants of state.

Internally, there is, in all honesty, no limit to the luxury of the Jeypore Museum. It revels in 'South Kensington' cases – of the approved pattern – that turn the beholder homesick, and South Kensington labels, whereon the description, measurements, and price of each object are fairly printed. These make savage one who knows how labelling is bungled in some of the Government Museums – our starved barns that are supposed to hold the economic exhibits, not of little states, but of great provinces.

The floors are of dark red chunam, overlaid with a discreet and silent matting; the doors, where they are not plate glass, are of carved wood, no two alike, hinged by sumptuous brass hinges on to marble jambs and opening without noise. On the carved marble pillars of each hall are fixed revolving cases of the South Kensington pattern to show textile fabrics, gold lace, and the like. In the recesses of the walls are more cases, and on the railing of the gallery that runs round each of the three great central rooms, are fixed low cases to hold natural history specimens and wax models of fruits and vegetables.

Hear this, Governments of India from the Punjab to Madras! The doors come true to the jamb, the cases, which have been through a hot weather, are neither warped nor cracked, nor are there unseemly tallow drops and flaws in the glasses. The maroon cloth, on or against which the exhibits are placed, is of close texture, untouched by the moth, neither stained nor meagre nor sun-faded; the revolving cases revolve freely without rattling; there is not a speck of dust from one end of the building to the other, because the menial staff are numerous enough to keep everything clean, and the curator's office is a veritable office – not a shed or a bathroom, or a loose box partitioned from the main building. These things are so because money has been spent on the museum, and it is now a rebuke to all other museums in India from Calcutta downwards. Whether it is not too good to be buried away in a native state is a question which envious men may raise and answer as they choose. Not long ago, the editor of a Bombay paper passed through it, but having the interests of the egocentric presidency before his eyes, dwelt more upon the idea of the building than its structural beauties; saying that Bombay, who professed a weakness for technical education, should be ashamed of herself. And he was quite right.

The system of the museum is complete in intention, as are its appointments in design. At present there are some fifteen thousand objects of art, covering a complete exposition of the arts, from enamels to pottery and from brassware to stone carving, of the State of Jeypore. They are compared with similar arts of other lands. Thus a Damio's sword – a gem of lacquer-plated silk and studwork – flanks the *tulwars* of Marwar and the *jezails* of Tonk; and reproductions of Persian and Russian brasswork stand side by side with the handicrafts of the pupils of the Jeypore School of Art. A photograph of His Highness the present Maharaja is set among the arms, which are the most prominent features of the first or metal room. As the villagers enter, they salaam reverently to the photo, and then move on slowly, with an evidently intelligent interest in what they see. Ruskin could describe the scene admirably – pointing out how reverence must precede the study of art, and how it is good for Englishmen and Rajputs alike to bow on occasion before Geisler's cap. They thumb the revolving cases of cloths do those rustics, and artlessly try to feel the texture through the protecting glass. The main object of the museum is avowedly provincial – to show the craftsman of Jeypore the best that his predecessors could do, and what foreign artists have done. In time – but the Curator of the museum has many schemes which will assuredly bear fruit in time, and it would be unfair to divulge them. Let those who doubt the thoroughness of a museum under one man's control, built, filled, and endowed with royal generosity – an institution perfectly independent of the Government of India – go and exhaustively visit Dr Hendley's charge at Jeypore. Like the man who made the building, he refuses to talk, and so the greater part of the work that he has in hand must be guessed at.

At one point, indeed, the curator was taken off his guard. A huge map of the kingdom showed in green the portions that had been brought under irrigation, while blue circles marked the towns that owned dispensaries. 'I want to bring every man in the State within twenty miles of a dispensary – and I've nearly done it,' said he. Then he checked himself, and went off to food grains in little bottles as being neutral and colourless things. Envy is forced to admit that the arrangement of the museum – far too important a matter to be explained off-hand – is continental in its character, and has a definite end and bearing – a trifle omitted by many institutions other than museums. But – in fine, what can one say of a collection whose very labels are gilt-edged! Shameful extravagance? Nothing of the kind – only finish, perfectly in keeping with the rest of the fittings – a finish that we in *kutcha* India have failed to catch.

From the Museum go out through the city to the Maharaja's Palace – skilfully avoiding the man who would show you the Maharaja's European billiard room – and wander through a wilderness of sunlit, sleepy courts, gay with paint and frescoes, till you reach an inner square, where smiling grey-bearded men squat at ease and play *chaupur* – just such a game as cost the Pandavs the fair Draupadi – with inlaid dice and gayly lacquered pieces. These ancients are very polite and will press you to play, but give no heed to them, for *chaupur* is an expensive game – expensive as quail fighting, when you have backed the wrong bird and the people are laughing at your inexperience. The Maharaja's Palace is gay, overwhelmingly rich in candelabra, painted ceilings, gilt mirrors, and other evidences of a too hastily assimilated civilisation; but, if the evidence of the ear can be trusted, the old, old game of intrigue goes on as merrily as of yore. A figure in saffron came out of a dark arch into the sunlight, almost falling into the arms of one in pink. 'Where have you come from?' 'I have been to see –' the name was unintelligible. 'That is a lie; you have *not!*' Then, across the court, someone laughed a low, croaking laugh. The pink and saffron figures separated as though they had been shot, and disappeared into separate boltholes. It was a curious little incident, and might have meant a great deal or just nothing at all. It distracted the attention of the ancients bowed above the *chaupur* cloth.

In the Palace gardens there is even a greater stillness than that about the courts, and here nothing of the West, unless a critical soul might take exception to the lamp posts. At the extreme end lies a lake-like tank swarming with *muggers*. It is reached through an opening under a block of zenana buildings. Remembering that all beasts by the palaces of kings or the temples of priests in this country would answer to the name of 'Brother', the Englishman cried with the voice of faith across the water. And the mysterious freemasonry did not fail. At the far end of the tank rose a ripple that grew and grew and grew like a thing in a nightmare, and became presently an aged *mugger*. As he neared the shore, there emerged, the green slime thick upon his eyelids, another beast, and the two together snapped at a cigar butt – the only reward for their courtesy. Then, disgusted, they sank stern first with a gentle sigh. Now a *mugger*'s sigh is the most suggestive sound in animal speech. It suggested first the zenana buildings overhead, the walled passes through the purple hills beyond, a horse that might clatter through the passes till he reached the Man Sagar Lake below the passes, and a boat that might row across the Man Sagar till it nosed the wall of the Palace tank, and then – then uprose the *mugger* with the filth upon his forehead and winked one horny eyelid – in truth he did! – and so supplied a fitting end to a foolish fiction of old days and things that might have been. But it must be unpleasant to live in a house whose base is washed by such a tank.

And so back through the chunamed courts, and among the gentle sloping paths between the orange trees, up to an entrance of the palace, guarded by two rusty brown dogs from Kabul, each big as a man, and each requiring a man's charpoy to sleep upon. Very gay was the front of the palace, very brilliant were the glimpses of the damask-couched, gilded rooms within, and very, very civilised were the lamp posts with Ram Singh's monogram, devised to look like V.R., at the bottom, and a coronet at the top. An unseen brass band among the orange bushes struck up the overture of the *Bronze Horse*. Those who know the music will see at once that that was the only tune which exactly and perfectly fitted the scene and its surroundings. It was a coincidence and a revelation.

In his time and when he was not fighting, Jey Singh, the second, who built the city, was a great astronomer – a royal Omar Khayyam, for he, like the tent-maker of Nishapur, reformed a calendar, and strove to wring their mysteries from the stars with instruments worthy of a king. But in the end he wrote that the goodness of the Almighty was above everything, and died, leaving his observatory to decay without the palace-grounds.

From the *Bronze Horse* to the grass-grown enclosure that holds the Yantr Samrat, or Prince of Dials, is rather an abrupt passage. Jey Singh built him a dial with a gnomon some ninety feet high, to throw a shadow against the sun, and the gnomon stands today, though there is grass in the kiosk at the top and the flight of steps up the hypotenuse is worn. He built also a zodiacal dial – twelve dials upon one platform – to find the moment of true noon at any time of the year, and hollowed out of the earth place for two hemispherical cups, cut by belts of stone, for comparative observations.

He made cups for calculating eclipses, and a mural quadrant and many other strange things of stone and mortar, of which people hardly know the names and but very little of the uses. Once, said a man in charge of two tiny elephants, *Indur* and *Har*, a Sahib came with the Viceroy, and spent eight days in the enclosure of the great neglected observatory, seeing and writing things in a book. But *he* understood *Sanskrit* – the Sanskrit upon the faces of the dials, and the meaning of the gnoma and pointers. Nowadays no one understands Sanskrit – not even the Pundits; but without doubt Jey Singh was a great man.

The hearer echoed the statement, though he knew nothing of astronomy, and of all the wonders in the observatory was only struck by the fact that the shadow of the Prince of Dials moved over its vast plate so quickly that it seemed as though Time, wroth at the insolence of Jey Singh, had loosed the Horses of the Sun and were sweeping everything – dainty palace gardens and ruinous instruments – into the darkness of eternal night. So he went away chased by the shadow on the dial, and returned to the hotel, where he found men who said – this must be a catchword of Globetrotters – that they were 'much pleased at' Amber. They further thought that 'house rent would be cheap in those parts', and sniggered over the witticism. There is a class of tourists, and a strangely large one, who individually never get farther than the 'much pleased' state under any circumstances. This same class of tourists, it has also been observed, are usually free with hackneyed puns, vapid phrases, and alleged or bygone jokes. Jey Singh, in spite of a few discreditable *laches*, was a temperate and tolerant man; but he would have hanged those Globetrotters in their trunk straps as high as the Yantr Samrat.

Next morning, in the grey dawn, the Englishman rose up and shook the sand of Jeypore from his feet, and went with Master Coryatt and Sir Thomas Roe to 'Adsmir', wondering whether a year in Jeypore would be sufficient to exhaust its interest, and why he had not gone out to the tombs of the dead Kings and the passes of Gulta and the fort of Motee Dungri. But what he wondered at most – knowing how many men who have in any way been connected with the birth of an institution, do, to the end of their days, continue to drag forward and exhume their labours and the honours that did *not* come to them – was the work of the two men who, together for years past, have been pushing Jeypore along the stone-dressed paths of civilisation, peace and comfort. 'Servants of the Raj' they called themselves, and surely they have served the Raj past all praise. The people in the city and the camel driver from the sandhills told of their work. They themselves held their peace as to what they had done, and, when pressed, referred – crowning baseness – to reports. Printed ones!

Touching the children of the sun and their city, and the hat-marked caste and their merits, and a good man's works in the wilderness.

It was worth a night's discomfort and revolver beds to sleep upon this city of the Suryavansi, hidden among the hills that encompass the great Pichola Lake. Truly, the King who governs today is wise in his determination to have no railroad to his capital. His predecessor was more or less enlightened, and had he lived a few years longer, would have brought the iron horse through the Dobarri – the green gate which is the entrance of the Girwa or girdle of hills around Udaipur; and, with the train, would have come the tourist who would have scratched his name upon the Temple of Garuda and laughed horse laughs upon the lake. Let us, therefore, be thankful that the capital of Mewar is hard to reach.

Each man in this land who has any claims to respectability walks armed, carrying his *tulwar* sheathed in his hand, or hung by a short sling of cotton passing over the shoulder, under his left armpit. His matchlock, or smooth bore, if he has one, is borne naked on the shoulder.

Now it is possible to carry any number of lethal weapons without being actually dangerous. An unhandy revolver, for instance, may be worn for years, and, at the end, accomplish nothing more noteworthy than the murder of its owner. But the Rajput's weapons are not meant for display. The Englishman caught a camel driver who talked to him in Mewari, which is a heathenish dialect, something like Multani to listen to; and the man, very gracefully and courteously, handed him his sword and matchlock, the latter a heavy stump-stock arrangement without pretence of sights. The blade was as sharp as a razor, and the gun in perfect working order. The coiled fuse on the stock was charred at the end, and the curled ram's horn powder horn opened as readily as a much-handled whisky flask. Unfortunately, ignorance of Mewari prevented conversation; so the camel driver resumed his accoutrements and jogged forward on his beast – a superb black one, with the short curled *hubshee* hair – while the Englishman went to the city, which is built on hills on the borders of the lake. By the way, everything in Udaipur is built on a hill. There is no level ground in the place, except the Durbar Gardens, of which more hereafter. Because colour holds the eye more than form, the first thing noticeable was neither temple nor fort, but an ever-recurring picture, painted in the rudest form of native art, of a man on horseback armed with a lance, charging an elephant-of-war. As a rule, the elephant was depicted on one side the house door and the rider on the other. There was no representation of an army behind. The figures stood alone upon the whitewash on house and wall and gate, again and again and again. A highly intelligent priest grunted that it was a picture; a private of the Maharana's regular army suggested that it was an elephant; while a wheat seller, his sword at his side, was equally certain that it was a Raja. Beyond that point, his knowledge did not go. The explanation of the picture is this. In the days when Raja Maun of Amber put his sword at Akbar's service and won for him great kingdoms, Akbar sent an army against Mewar, whose then ruler was Pertap Singh, most famous of all the princes of Mewar. Selim, Akbar's son, led the army of the Toork; the Rajputs met them at the pass of Huldighat and fought till one-half of their band was slain. Once, in the press of battle, Pertap on his great horse, Chytak, came within striking distance of Selim's elephant, and slew the mahout, but Selim escaped, to become Jehangir afterwards, and the Rajputs were broken. That was three hundred years ago, and men have reduced the picture to a sort of diagram that the painter dashes in, in a few minutes, without, it would seem, knowing what he is commemorating.

Thinking of these things, the Englishman made shift to get to the city, and presently came to a tall gate, the gate of the Sun, on which the elephant spikes, that he had seen rotted with rust at Amber, were new and pointed and effective. The city gates are said to be shut at night, and there is a story of a Viceroy's Guard of Honour which arrived before daybreak, being compelled to crawl ignominiously man by man through a little wicket gate, while the horses had to wait without till sunrise. But a civilised yearning for the utmost advantages of octroi, and not a fierce fear of robbery and wrong, is at the bottom of the continuance of this custom. The walls of the city are loopholed for musketry, but there seem to be no mounting for guns, and the moat without the walls is dry and gives cattle pasture. Coarse rubble in concrete faced with stone makes the walls moderately strong.

Internally, the city is surprisingly clean, though with the exception of the main street, paved after the fashion of Jullundur, of which, men say, the pavement was put down in the time of Alexander and worn by myriads of naked feet into deep barrels and grooves. In the case of Udaipur, the feet of the passengers have worn the rock veins that crop out everywhere, smooth and shiny; and in the rains the narrow gullies must spout like fire hoses. The people have been untouched by cholera for four years, proof that Providence looks after those who do not look after themselves, for Neemuch Cantonment, a hundred miles away, suffered grievously last summer. 'And what do you make in Udaipur?' 'Swords,' said the man in the shop, throwing down an armful of *tulwars*, *kuttars*, and *khandas* on the stones. 'Do you want any? Look here!' Hereat, he took up one of the commoner swords and flourished it in the sunshine. Then he bent it double, and, as it sprang straight, began to make it 'speak'. Arm vendors in Udaipur are a sincere race, for they sell to people who really use their wares. The man in the shop was rude – distinctly so. His first flush of professional enthusiasm abated, he took stock of the Englishman and said calmly: 'What do *you* want with a sword?' Then he picked up his goods and retreated, while certain small boys, who deserved a smacking, laughed riotously from the coping of a little temple hard by. Swords seem to be the sole manufacture of the place. At least, none of the inhabitants the Englishman spoke to could think of any other.

There is a certain amount of personal violence in and about the State, or elsewhere would be the good of the weapons? There are occasionally dacoities more or less important; but these are not often heard of, and, indeed, there is no special reason why they should be dragged into the light of an unholy publicity, for the land governs itself in its own way, and is always in its own way, which is by no means ours, very happy. The Thakurs live, each in his own castle on some rock-faced hill, much as they lived in the days of Tod; though their chances of distinguishing themselves, except in the school, and dispensary line, are strictly limited. Nominally, they pay *chutoond*, or a sixth of their revenues to the state, and are under feudal obligations to supply their head with so many horsemen per thousand rupees; but whether the *chutoond* justifies its name and what is the exact extent of the 'tail' leviable, they, and perhaps the Rajputana Agency, alone know. They are quiet, give no trouble except to the wild boar, and personally are magnificent men to look at. The Rajput shows his breeding in his hands and feet, which are almost disproportionately small, and as well shaped as those of a woman. His stirrups and sword handles are even more unusable by Westerns than those elsewhere in India, whereas the Bhil's knife handle gives as large a grip as an English one. Now the little Bhil is an aborigine, which is humiliating to think of. His tongue, which may frequently be heard in the city, seems to possess some variant of the Zulu click, which gives it a weird and unearthly character. From the main gate of the city the Englishman climbed uphill towards the Palace and the Jugdesh Temple built by one Juggat Singh at the beginning of the last century. This building must be – but ignorance is a bad guide – Jain in character. From basement to the stone socket of the temple flagstaff, it is carved in high relief with elephants, men, gods, and monsters in friezes of wearying profusion.

The management of the temple have daubed a large portion of the building with whitewash, for which their revenues should be 'cut' for a year or two. The main shrine holds a large brazen image of Garuda, and, in the corners of the courtyard of the main pile, are shrines to Mahadeo, and the jovial, pot-bellied Ganesh. There is no repose in this architecture, and the entire effect is one of repulsion; for the clustered figures of man and brute seem always on the point of bursting into unclean, wriggling life. But it may be that the builders of this form of house desired to put the fear of all their many gods into the hearts of the worshippers. From the temple whose steps are worn smooth by the feet of men, and whose courts are full of the faint smell of stale flowers and old incense, the Englishman went to the palaces which crown the highest hill overlooking the city. Here, too, whitewash had been unsparingly applied, but the excuse was that the stately fronts and the pierced screens were built of a perishable stone which needed protection against the weather. One projecting window in the facade of the main palace had been treated with Minton tiles. Luckily it was too far up the wall for anything more than the colour to be visible, and the pale blue against the pure white was effective.

A picture of Ganesh looks out over the main courtyard, which is entered by a triple gate, and hard by is the place where the King's elephants fight over a low masonry wall. In the side of the hill on which the palaces stand is built stabling for horses and elephants – proof that the architects of old must have understood their business thoroughly. The palace is not a 'show place', and, consequently, the Englishman did not see much of the interior. But he passed through open gardens with tanks and pavilions, very cool and restful, till he came suddenly upon the Pichola Lake, and forgot altogether about the palace. He found a sheet of steel-blue water, set in purple and grey hills, bound in, on one side, by marble bunds, the fair white walls of the palace, and the grey, timeworn ones of the city; and, on the other, fading away through the white of shallow water, and the soft green of weed, marsh, and rank-pastured river-field, into the land.

To enjoy open water thoroughly, live for a certain number of years barred from anything better than the yearly swell and shrinkage of one of the Five Rivers, and then come upon two and a half miles of solid, restful lake, with a cool wind blowing off it and little waves spitting against the piers of a veritable, albeit hideously ugly, boathouse. On the faith of an exile from the Sea, you will not stay long among Palaces, be they never so lovely, or in little rooms panelled with Dutch tiles.

And here follows a digression. There is no life so good as the life of a loafer who travels by rail and road; for all things and all people are kind to him. From the chill miseries of a dak-bungalow where they slew one hen with as much parade as the French guillotined Pranzini, to the well-ordered sumptuousness of the residency, was a step bridged over by kindly and unquestioning hospitality. So it happened that the Englishman was not only able to go upon the lake in a soft-cushioned boat, with everything handsome about him, but might, had he chosen, have killed wild duck with which the lake swarms.

The mutter of water under a boat's nose was a pleasant thing to hear once more. Starting at the head of the lake, he found himself shut out from sight of the main sheet of water in a loch bounded by a sunk, broken bund to steer across which was a matter of some nicety. Beyond that lay a second pool, spanned by a narrow-arched bridge built, men said, long before the City of the Rising Sun, which is little more than three hundred years old. The bridge connects the city with Brahmapura – a whiter walled enclosure filled with many Brahmins and ringing with the noise of their conches. Beyond the bridge, the body of the lake, with the city running down to it, comes into full view; and Providence has arranged for the benefit of such as delight in colours, that the Rajputni shall wear the most striking tints that she can buy in the bazaars, in order that she may beautify the ghats where she comes to bathe.

The bathing ledge at the foot of the city wall was lighted with women clad in raw vermilion, dull red, indigo and sky-blue, saffron and pink and turquoise; the water faithfully doubling everything. But the first impression was of the unreality of the sight, for the Englishman found himself thinking of the Simla Fine Arts Exhibition and the over-daring amateurs who had striven to reproduce scenes such as these. Then a woman rose up, and clasping her hands behind her head, looked at the passing boat, and the ripples spread out from her waist, in blinding white silver, far across the water. As a picture, a daringly insolent picture, it was superb.

The boat turned aside to shores where huge turtles were lying, and a stork had built her a nest, big as a haycock, in a withered tree, and a bevy of coots were flapping and gabbling in the weeds or between great leaves of the *Victoria regia* – an 'escape' from the State Gardens. Here were divers and waders, kingfishers and snaky-necked birds of the cormorant family, but no duck. They had seen the guns in the boat and were flying to and fro in companies across the lake, or settling – wise things! – in the glare of the sun on the water. The lake was swarming with them, but they seemed to know exactly how far a twelve-bore would carry. Perhaps their knowledge had been gained from the Englishman at the Residency. Later, as the sun left the lake, and the hills began to glow like opals, the boat made her way to the shallow side of the lake, through fields of water grass and dead lotus raffle that rose as high as the bows, and clung lovingly about the rudder, and parted with the noise of silk when it is torn. There she waited for the fall of twilight when the duck would come home to bed, and the Englishman sprawled upon the cushions in deep content and laziness, as he looked across to where two marble palaces floated upon the waters, and saw all the glory and beauty of the city, and wondered whether Tod, in cocked hat and stiff stock, had ever come shooting among the reeds, and, if so, how in the world he had ever managed to bowl over…

'Duck and drake, by Jove! Confiding beasts, weren't they. Hi! Lalla, jump out and get them!' It was a brutal thing, this double-barrelled murder perpetrated in the silence of the marsh when the kingly wild duck came back from his wanderings with his mate at his side, but – but – the birds were very good to eat.

If the Venetian owned the Pichola Sagar he might say with justice: 'See it and die.' But it is better to live and go to dinner, and strike into a new life – that of the men who bear the hat-mark on their brow as plainly as the well-born native carries the *trishul* of Shiva.

They are of the same caste as the toilers on the frontier – tough, bronzed men, with wrinkles at the corners of the eyes, gotten by looking across much sun glare. When they would speak of horses they mention Arab ponies, and their talk, for the most part, drifts Bombaywards, or to Abu, which is their Simla. By these things the traveller may see that he is far away from the presidency; and will presently learn that he is in a land where the railway is an incident and not an indispensable luxury. Folk tell strange stories of drives in bullock carts in the rains, of breakdowns in nullahs fifty miles from everywhere, and of elephants that used to sink for rest and refreshment halfway across swollen streams. Every place here seems fifty miles from everywhere, and the legs of a horse are regarded as the only natural means of locomotion. Also, and this to the Indian Cockney, who is accustomed to the bleached or office man, is curious, there are to be found many veritable 'tiger-men' – not story-spinners, but such as have, in their wanderings from Bikaneer to Indore, dropped their tiger in the way of business. They are enthusiastic over princelings of little known fiefs, lords of austere estates perched on the tops of unthrifty hills, hard riders, and good sportsmen. And five, six, yes fully nine hundred miles to the northward, lives the sister branch of the same caste – the men who swear by Pathan, Biluch, and Brahui, with whom they have shot or broken bread.

There is a saying in Upper India that the more desolate the country, the greater the certainty of finding a Padre Sahib. The proverb seems to hold good in Udaipur, where the Scotch Presbyterian Mission have a post, and others at Todgarh to the north and elsewhere. To arrive, under Providence, at the cure of souls through the curing of bodies certainly seems the rational method of conversion; and this is exactly what the Missions are doing. Their Padre in Udaipur is also an M.D., and of him a rather striking tale is told. Conceiving that the City could bear another hospital in addition to the State one, he took furlough, went home, and there, by crusade and preaching, raised sufficient money for the scheme, so that none might say that he was beholden to the State. Returning, he built his hospital, a very model of neatness and comfort, and, opening the operation book, announced his readiness to see anyone and everyone who was sick. How the call was and is now responded to, the dry records of that book will show; and the name of the Padre Sahib is honoured, as these ears have heard, throughout Udaipur and far around. The faith that sends a man into the wilderness, and the secular energy which enables him to cope with an ever-growing demand for medical aid, must, in time, find their reward. If patience and unwearying self sacrifice carry any merit, they should do so soon. Today the people are willing enough to be healed, and the general influence of the Padre Sahib is very great. But beyond that... Still it was impossible to judge aright.

Proves conclusively the existence of the dark tower visited by Childe Rolande, and of 'bogey' who frightens children.

The Gamberi River – clear as a trout-stream – runs through the waste round Chitoor, and is spanned by an old bridge, very solid and massive, said to have been built before the sack of Ala-ud-din. The bridge is in the middle of the stream – the floods have raced round either end of it – and is reached by a steeply sloping stone causeway. From the bridge to the new town of Chitoor, which lies at the foot of the hill, runs a straight and well-kept road, flanked on either side by the scattered remnants of old houses, and, here and there, fallen temples. The road, like the bridge, is no new thing, and is wide enough for twenty horsemen to ride abreast.

New Chitoor is a very dirty, and apparently thriving, little town, full of grain-merchants and sellers of arms. The ways are barely wide enough for the elephant of dignity and the little brown babies of impudence. The Englishman went through, always on a slope painfully accentuated by Gerowlia who, with all possible respect to her years, must have been a baggage-animal and no true sahib's mount. Let the local Baedeker speak for a moment: 'The ascent to Chitor, which begins from within the southeast angle of the town, is nearly a mile to the upper gate, with a slope of about 1 in 15. There are two zigzag bends, and on the three portions thus formed, are seven gates, of which one, however, has only the basement left.' This is the language of fact, which, very properly, leaves out of all account the Genius of the Place who sits at the gate nearest the new city and is with the sightseer throughout. The first impression of repulsion and awe is given by a fragment of tumbled sculpture close to a red daubed *lingam*, near the Padal Pol or lowest gate. It is a piece of frieze, and the figures of the men are worn nearly smooth by time. What is visible is finely and frankly obscene to an English mind.

The road is protected on the cliff side by a thick stone wall, loopholed for musketry, one aperture to every two feet, between fifteen and twenty feet high. This wall is being repaired throughout its length by the Maharana of Udaipur. On the hillside, among the boulders, loose stones, and *dhak*-scrub, lips stone wreckage that must have come down from the brown bastions above.

As Gerowlia laboured up the stone-shod slope, the Englishman wondered how much life had flowed down this sluice of battles, and been lost at the Padal Pol – the last and lowest gate – where, in the old days, the besieging armies put their best and bravest battalions. Once at the head of the lower slope, there is a clear run-down of a thousand yards with no chance of turning aside either to the right or left. Even as he wondered, he was brought abreast of two stone chhatris, each carrying a red daubed stone. They were the graves of two very brave men, Jeemal of Bedmore, and Kalla, who fell in Akbar's sack fighting like Rajputs. Read the story of their deaths, and learn what manner of warriors they were. Their graves were all that spoke openly of the hundreds of struggles on the lower slope where the fight was always fiercest.

At last, after half an hour's climb, the main gate, the Ram Pol, was gained, and the Englishman passed into the City of Chitor and – then and there formed a resolution, since broken, not to write one word about it for fear that he should be set down as a babbling and a gushing enthusiast. Objects of archaeological interest are duly described in an admirable little book of Chitoor which, after one look, the Englishman abandoned. One cannot 'do' Chitoor with a guidebook. The Chaplain of the English Mission to Jehangir said the best that was to be said, when he described the place three hundred years ago, writing quaintly: 'Chitoor, an ancient great kingdom, the chief city so called which standeth on a mighty high hill, flat on the top, walled about at the least ten English miles. There appear to this day above a hundred churches ruined and divers fair palaces which are lodged in like manner among their ruins, as many Englishmen by the observation have guessed. Its chief inhabitants today are Zum and Ohim, birds and wild beasts, but the stately ruins thereof give a shadow of its beauty while it flourished in its pride.' Gerowlia struck into a narrow pathway, forcing herself through garden trees and disturbing the peacocks. An evil guide-man on the ground waved his hand, and began to speak; but was silenced. The death of Amber was as nothing to the death of Chitoor – a body whence the life had been driven by riot and the sword. Men had parcelled the gardens of her palaces and the courtyards of her temples into fields; and cattle grazed among the remnants of the shattered tombs. But over all – over rent and bastion, split temple-wall, pierced roof, and prone pillar – lay the 'shadow of its beauty while it flourished in its pride'. The Englishman walked into a stately palace of many rooms, where the sunlight streamed in through wall and roof, and up crazy stone stairways, held together, it seemed, by the marauding trees. In one bastion, a wind-sown peepul had wrenched a thick slab clear of the wall, but held it tight pressed in a crook of a branch, as a man holds down a fallen enemy under his elbow, shoulder, and forearm. In another place, a strange, uncanny wind sprung from nowhere, was singing all alone among the pillars of what may have been a Hall of Audience. The Englishman wandered so far in one palace that he came to an almost black-dark room, high up in a wall, and said proudly to himself: 'I must be the first man who has been here'; meaning no harm or insult to anyone. But he tripped and fell, and as he put out his hands, he felt that the stairs had been worn hollow and smooth by the thread of innumerable naked feet. Then he was afraid, and came away very quickly, stepping delicately over fallen friezes and bits of sculptured men, so as not to offend the Dead; and was mightily relieved when he recovered his elephant and allowed the guide to take him to Kumbha Rana's Tower of Victory.

This stands, like all things in Chitoor, among ruins, but time and the other enemies have been good to it. It is a Jain edifice, nine storeys high, crowned atop – was this designed insult or undesigned repair? – with a purely Mahometan dome, where the pigeons and the bats live. Excepting this blemish, the Tower of Victory is nearly as fair as when it left the hands of the builder whose name has not been handed down to us. It is to be observed here that the first, or more ruined, Tower of Victory, built in Alluji's days, when Chitoor was comparatively young, was raised by some pious Jain as proof of conquest over things spiritual. The second tower is more worldly in intent.

Those who care to look may find elsewhere a definition of its architecture and its more striking peculiarities. It was in kind, but not in degree, like the Jugdesh Temple at Udaipur, and, as it exceeded it in magnificence, so its effect upon the mind was more intense. The confusing intricacy of the figures with which it was wreathed from top to bottom, the recurrence of the one calm face, the God enthroned, holding the Wheel of the Law, and the appalling lavishness of decoration, all worked toward the instilment of fear and aversion.

Surely this must have been one of the objects of the architect. The tower, in the arrangement of its stairways, is like the interior of a Chinese carved ivory puzzle-ball. The idea given is that, even while you are ascending, you are wrapping yourself deeper and deeper in the tangle of a mighty maze. Add to this the half-light, the throning armies of sculptured figures, the mad profusion of design splashed as impartially upon the undersides of the stone window-slabs as upon the door-beam of the threshold – add, most abhorrent of all, the slippery sliminess of the walls always worn smooth by naked men, and you will understand that the tower is not a soothing place to visit. The Englishman fancied presumptuously that he had, in a way, grasped the builder's idea; and when he came to the top storey and sat among the pigeons his theory was this: to attain power, wrote the builder of old, in sentences of fine stone, it is necessary to pass through all sorts of close-packed horrors, treacheries, battles, and insults, in darkness and without knowledge whether the road leads upward or into a hopeless *cul-de-sac*. Kumbha Rana must many times have climbed to the top storey, and looked out toward the uplands of Malwa on the one side and his own great Mewar on the other, in the days when all the rock hummed with life and the clatter of hooves upon the stony ways, and Mahmoud of Malwa was safe in hold. How he must have swelled with pride – fine insolent pride of life and rule and power – power not only to break things but to compel such builders as those who piled the tower to his royal will! There was no decoration in the top storey to bewilder or amaze – nothing but well-grooved stone-slabs, and a boundless view fit for kings who traced their ancestry –

From times when forth from the sunlight, the first of our
Kings came down,
And had the earth for his footstool, and wore the stars for
his crown.

The builder had left no mark behind him – not even a mark on the threshold of the door, or a sign in the head of the topmost step. The Englishman looked in both places, believing that those were the places generally chosen for mark-cutting. So he sat and meditated on the beauties of kingship and the unholiness of Hindu art, and what power a shadowland of lewd monstrosities had upon those who believed in it, and what Lord Dufferin, who is the nearest approach to a king in this India, must have thought when aide-de-camps clanked after him up the narrow steps. But the day was wearing, and he came down – in both senses – and, in his descent, the carven things on every side of the tower, and above and below, once more took hold of and perverted his fancy, so that he arrived at the bottom in a frame of mind eminently fitted for a descent into the Gau-Mukh, which is nothing more terrible than a little spring, falling into a reservoir, in the side of the hill.

He stumbled across more ruins and passed between tombs of dead Ranis, till he came to a flight of steps, built out and cut out from rock, going down as far as he could see into a growth of trees on a terrace below him. The stone of the steps had been worn and polished by the terrible naked feet till it showed its markings clearly as agate; and where the steps ended in a rock-slope, there was a visible glair, a great snail-track, upon the rocks. It was hard to keep safe footing upon the sliminess. The air was thick with the sick smell of stale incense, and grains of rice were scattered upon the steps. But there was no one to be seen. Now this in itself was not specially alarming; but the Genius of the Place must be responsible for making it so. The Englishman slipped and bumped on the rocks, and arrived, more suddenly than he desired, upon the edge of a dull blue tank, sunk between walls of timeless masonry. In a slabbed-in recess, water was pouring through a shapeless stone gargoyle, into a trough; which trough again dripped into the tank. Almost under the little trickle of water, was the loathsome Emblem of Creation, and there were flowers and rice around it. Water was trickling from a score of places in the cut face of the hill; oozing between the edges of the steps and welling up between the stone slabs of the terrace. Trees sprouted in the sides of the tank and hid its surroundings. It seemed as though the descent had led the Englishman, firstly, two thousand years away from his own century, and secondly, into a trap, and that he would fall off the polished stones into the stinking tank, or that the Gau-Mukh would continue to pour water until the tank rose up and swamped him, or that some of the stone slabs would fall forward and crush him flat.

Then he was conscious of remembering, with peculiar and unnecessary distinctness, that, from the Gau-Mukh, a passage led to the subterranean chambers in which the fair Pudmini and her handmaids had slain themselves. And, that Tod had written and the Station-master at Chitoor had said, that some sort of devil, or ghoul, or Something, stood at the entrance of that approach. All of which was a nightmare bred in full day and folly to boot; but it was the fault of the Genius of the Place, who made the Englishman feel that he had done a great wrong in trespassing into the very heart and soul of all Chitoor. And, behind him, the Gau-Mukh guggled and choked like a man in his death-throe. The Englishman endured as long as he could – about two minutes. Then it came upon him that he must go quickly out of this place of years and blood – must get back to the afternoon sunshine, and Gerowlia, and the dak-bungalow with the French bedstead. He desired no archaeological information, he wished to take no notes, and, above all, he did not care to look behind him, where stood the reminder that he was no better than the beasts that perish. But he had to cross the smooth, worn rocks, and he felt their sliminess through his bootsoles. It was as though he were treading on the soft, oiled skin of a Hindu. As soon as the steps gave refuge, he floundered up them, and so came out of the Gau-Mukh, bedewed with that perspiration which follows alike on honest toil or – childish fear.

'This,' said he to himself, 'is absurd!' and sat down on the fallen top of a temple to review the situation. But the Gau-Mukh had disappeared. He could see the dip in the ground and the beginning of the steps, but nothing more.

Perhaps it was absurd. It undoubtedly appeared so, later. Yet there was something uncanny about it all. It was not exactly a feeling of danger or pain, but an apprehension of great evil.

In defence, it may be urged that there is moral, just as much as there is mine, choke-damp. If you get into a place laden with the latter you die, and if into the home of the former you… behave unwisely, as constitution and temperament prompt. If any man doubt this, let him sit for two hours in a hot sun on an elephant, stay half an hour in the Tower of Victory, and then go down into the Gau-Mukh, which, it must never be forgotten, is merely a set of springs 'three or four in number, issuing from the cliff face at cow-mouth carvings, now mutilated. The water, evidently percolating from the Hathi Kund above, falls first in an old pillared hall and thence into the masonry reservoir below, eventually, when abundant enough, supplying a little waterfall lower down.' That, Gentlemen and Ladies, on the honour of one who has been frightened of the dark in broad daylight, is the Gau-Mukh, as though photographed.

The Englishman regained Gerowlia and demanded to be taken away, but Gerowlia's driver went forward instead and showed him a new Mahal just built by the present Maharana. Carriage drives, however, do not consort well with Chitoor and the 'shadow of her ancient beauty'. The return journey, past temple after temple and palace upon palace, began in the failing light, and Gerowlia was still blundering up and down narrow bypaths – for she possessed all an old woman's delusion as to the slimness of her waist when the twilight fell, and the smoke from the town below began to creep up the brown flanks of Chitoor, and the jackals howled. Then the sense of desolation, which had been strong enough in all conscience in the sunshine, began to grow and grow.

Near the Ram Pol there was some semblance of a town with living people in it, and a priest sat in the middle of the road and howled aloud upon his gods, until a little boy came and laughed in his face and he went away grumbling. This touch was deeply refreshing; in the contemplation of it, the Englishman clean forgot that he had overlooked the gathering in of materials for an elaborate statistical, historical, geographical account of Chitoor. All that remained to him was a shuddering reminiscence of the Gau-Mukh and two lines of the 'Holy Grail',

And up into the sounding halls he passed,
But nothing in the sounding halls he saw.

Post Scriptum – There was something very uncanny about the Genius of the Place. He dragged an ease-loving egotist out of the French bedstead with the gilt knobs at head and foot, into a more than usually big folly – nothing less than a seeing of Chitoor by moonlight. There was no possibility of getting Gerowlia out of *her* bed, and a mistrust of the Maharana's soldiery who in the daytime guarded the gates, prompted the Englishman to avoid the public way, and scramble straight up the hillside, along an attempt at a path which he had noted from Gerowlia's back. There was no one to interfere, and nothing but an infinity of pestilent nullahs and loose stones to check. Owls came out and hooted at him, and animals ran about in the dark and made uncouth noises. It was an idiotic journey, and it ended – Oh, horror! in that unspeakable Gau-Mukh – this time entered from the opposite or brushwooded side, as far as could be made out in the dusk and from the chuckle of the water which, by night, was peculiarly malevolent.

Escaping from this place, crab-fashion, the Englishman crawled into Chitoor and sat upon a flat tomb till the moon, a very inferior and second-hand one, rose, and turned the city of the dead into a city of scurrying ghouls – in sobriety, jackals. The ruins took strange shapes and shifted in the half-light and cast objectionable shadows.

It was easy enough to fill the rock with the people of old times, and a very beautiful account of Chitoor restored, made out by the help of Tod, and bristling with the names of the illustrious dead, would undoubtedly have been written, had not a woman, a living breathing woman, stolen out of a temple – what was she doing in that galley? – and screamed in piercing and public-spirited fashion. The Englishman got off the tomb and departed rather more noisily than a jackal; feeling for the moment that he was not much better. Somebody opened a door with a crash, and a man cried out: 'Who is there?' But the cause of the disturbance was, for his sins, being most horribly scratched by some thorny scrub over the edge of the hill – there are no bastions worth speaking of near the Gau-Mukh – and the rest was partly rolling, partly scrambling, and mainly bad language.

When you are too lucky sacrifice something, a beloved pipe for choice, to Ganesh. The Englishman has seen Chitoor by moonlight – not the best moonlight truly, but the watery glare of a nearly spent moon – and his sacrifice to Luck is this. He will never try to describe what he has seen – but will keep it as a love-letter, a thing for one pair of eyes only – a memory that few men today can be sharers in. And does he, through this fiction, evade insulting, by pen and ink, a scene as lovely, wild, and unmatchable as any that mortal eyes have been privileged to rest upon?

An intelligent and discriminating public are perfectly at liberty to form their own opinions.

A king's house and country. Further consideration of the hat-marked caste.

The hospitality that spreads tables in the wilderness, and shifts the stranger from the back of the hired camel into a two-horse victoria, must be experienced to be appreciated.

To those unacquainted with the peculiarities of the native-trained horse, this advice may be worth something. Sit as far back as ever you can, and, if Oriental courtesy have put an English bit and bridoon in a mouth by education intended for a spiked curb, leave the whole contraption alone. Once acquainted with the comparative smoothness of English ironmongery, your mount will grow frivolous. In which event a four-pound steeple-chase saddle, accepted through sheer shame, offers the very smallest amount of purchase to untrained legs.

The Englishman rode up to the Fort, and by the way learnt all these things and many more. He was provided with a racking, female horse who swept the gullies of the city by dancing sideways.

The road to the Fort, which stands on the Hill of Strife, wound in and out of sixty-foot hills, with a skilful avoidance of all shade; and this was at high noon, when puffs of heated air blew from the rocks on all sides. 'What must the heat be in May?' The Englishman's companion was a cheery Brahmin, who wore the lightest of turbans and sat the smallest of neat little country-breds. 'Awful!' said the Brahmin. 'But not so bad as in the district. Look there!' and he pointed from the brow of a bad eminence, across the quivering heat-haze, to where the white sand faded into bleach blue sky and the horizon was shaken and tremulous. 'It's very bad in summer. Would knock you – oh yes – all to smash, but *we* are accustomed to it.' A rock-strewn hill, about half a mile, as the crow flies, from the Fort was pointed out as the place whence, at the beginning of this century, the Pretender Sowae besieged Raja Maun for five months, but could make no headway against his foe. One gun of the enemy's batteries specially galled the Fort, and the Jodhpur King offered a village to any of his gunners who should dismount it. 'It was smashed,' said the Brahmin. 'Oh yes, all to pieces.' Practically, the city which lies below the Fort is indefensible, and during the many wars of Marwar has generally been taken up by the assailants without resistance.

Entering the Fort by the Jeypore Gate, and studiously refraining from opening his umbrella, the Englishman found shadow and coolth, took off his hat to the tun-bellied, trunk-nosed God of Good-Luck who had been very kind to him in his wanderings, and sat down near half a dozen of the Maharaja's guns bearing the mark, 'A. Broome, Cossipore, 1857', or 'G. Hutchinson, Cossipore, 1838'. Now rock and masonry are so curiously blended in this great pile that he who walks through it loses sense of being among buildings. It is as though he walked through mountain-gorges. The stone-paved, inclined planes, and the tunnel-like passages driven under a hundred feet height of buildings, increase this impression. In many places the wall and rock runs up unbroken by any window for forty feet.

It would be a week's work to pick out even roughly the names of the dead who have added to the buildings, or to describe the bewildering multiplicity of courts and ranges of rooms; and, in the end, the result would be as satisfactory as an attempt to describe a nightmare. It is said that the rock on which the Fort stands is four miles in circuit, but no man yet has dared to estimate the size of the city that they call the Palace, or the mileage of its ways. Ever since Ras Joda, four hundred years ago, listened to the voice of a *Jogi*, and leaving Mundore built his eyrie on the 'Bird's nest' as the Hill of Strife was called, the palaces have grown and thickened. Even today the builders are still at work. Takht Singh, the present ruler's predecessor, built royally. An incomplete bastion and a Hall of Flowers are among the works of his pleasure. Hidden away behind a mighty wing of carved red sandstone lie rooms set apart for Viceroys, Durbar Halls and dinner rooms without end. A gentle gloom covers the evidences of the catholic taste of the state in articles of 'bigotry and virtue'; but there is enough light to show the *raison d'être* of the men who wait in the dak-bungalow. And, after all, what is the use of royalty in these days if a man may not take delight in the pride of the eye? Kumbha Rana, the great man of Chitor, fought like a Rajput, but he had an instinct which made him build the Tower of Victory at, who knows what cost of money and life. The fighting-instinct thrown back upon itself must have some sort of outlet; and a merciful Providence wisely ordains that the Kings of the East in the nineteenth century shall take pleasure in shopping on an imperial scale. Dresden China snuffboxes, mechanical engines, electroplated fish-slicers, musical boxes, and gilt blown-glass Christmas-tree balls do not go well with the splendours of a Palace that might have been built by Titans and coloured by the morning sun. But there are excuses to be made for kings who have no fighting to do.

In one of the higher bastions stands a curious specimen of one of the earliest *mitrailleuses* – a cumbrous machine carrying twenty gun-barrels in two rows, which small-arm fire is flanked by two tiny cannon. As a muzzle-loading implement its value after the first discharge would be insignificant; but the soldiers lounging by assured the Englishman that it had done good service in its time.

A man may spend a long hour in the upper tiers of the Palaces, but still far from the rooftops, in looking out across the desert. There are Englishmen in these wastes, who say gravely that there is nothing so fascinating as the sand of Bikanir and Marwar. 'You see,' explained an enthusiast of the Hat-marked Caste, 'you are not shut in by roads, and you can go just as you please. And, somehow, it grows upon you as you get used to it, and you end, y'know, by falling in love with the place.' Look steadily from the palace westward where the city with its tanks and serais is spread at your feet, and you will, in a lame way, begin to understand the fascination of the Desert which, by those who have felt it, is said to be even stronger than the fascination of the road. The city is of red sandstone and dull and sombre to look at. Beyond it, where the white sand lies, the country is dotted with camels limping into the Ewigkeit or coming from the same place. Trees appear to be strictly confined to the suburbs of the city. Very good. If you look long enough across the sands, while a voice in your ear is telling you of half-buried cities, old as old Time, and wholly unvisited by Sahibs, of districts where the white man is unknown, and of the wonders of faraway Jeysulmir ruled by a half-distraught king, sand-locked and now smitten by a terrible food and water famine, you will, if it happen that you are of a sedentary and civilised nature, experience a new emotion – will be conscious of a great desire to take one of the lobbing camels and get away into the desert, away from the last touch of today, to meet the past face to face. Some day a novelist will exploit the unknown land from the Rann, where the wild ass breeds, northward and eastward, till he comes to the Indus.

But the officials of Marwar do not call their country a desert. On the contrary, they administer it very scientifically and raise, as has been said, about thirty-eight lakhs from it. To come back from the influence and the possible use of the desert to more prosaic facts. Read quickly a rough record of things in modern Marwar. The old is drawn in Tod, who speaks the truth. The Maharaja's right hand in the work of the State is Maharaj Sir Pertab Singh, Prime Minister ADC to the Prince of Wales, capable of managing the Marwari who intrigues like a – Marwari, equally capable, as has been seen, of moving in London Society, and Colonel of a newly raised crack cavalry corps. The Englishman would have liked to have seen him, but he was away in the desert somewhere, either marking a boundary or looking after a succession case. Not very long ago, as the Setts of Ajmer knew well, there was a State debt of fifty lakhs. This has now been changed into a surplus of three lakhs, and the revenue is growing. Also, the simple Dacoit who used to enjoy himself very pleasantly, has been put into a department, and the Thug with him.

Consequently, for the department takes a genuine interest in this form of *shikar*, and the gaol leg-irons are not too light, dacoities have been reduced to such an extent that men say 'you may send a woman, with her ornaments upon her, from Sojat to Phalodi, and she will not lose a nose-ring'. Again, and this in a Rajput State is an important matter, the boundaries of nearly every village in Marwar have been demarcated, and boundary fights, in which both sides preferred small-arm fire to the regulation club, are unknown. The open-handed system of giving away villages had raised a large and unmannerly crop of *jaghirdars*. These have been taken up and brought in hand by Sir Pertab Singh, to the better order of the State.

A Punjabi Sirdar, Har Dyal Singh, has reformed, or made rather, Courts on the Civil and Criminal Side; and his hand is said to be found in a good many sweepings out of old corners. It must always be borne in mind that everything that has been done, was carried through over and under unlimited intrigue, for Jodhpur is a Native State. Intrigue must be met with intrigue by all except Gordons or demi-gods; and it is curious to hear how a reduction in tariff, or a smoothing out of some tangled court, had to be worked by shift and byway. The tales are comic, but not for publication. Howbeit, Har Dyal Singh got his training in part under the Punjab Government, and in part in a little Native State far away in the Himalayas, where intrigue is not altogether unknown. To the credit of the 'Pauper Province' be it said, it is not easy to circumvent a Punjabi. The details of his work would be dry reading. The result of it is good, and there is justice in Marwar, and order and firmness in its administration.

Naturally, the land revenue is the most interesting thing in Marwar from an administrative point of view. The basis of it is a tank about the size of a swimming-bath, with a catchment of several hundred square yards, draining through leeped channels. When God sends the rain, the people of the village drink from the tank. When the rains fail, as they failed this year, they take to their wells, which are brackish and breed guinea-worm.

For these reasons the revenue, like the Republic of San Domingo, is never alike for two years running. There are no canal questions to harry the authorities; but the fluctuations are enormous. Under the Aravallis the soil is good: further north they grow millet and pasture cattle, though, said a Revenue Officer cheerfully, 'God knows what the brutes find to eat.' A propos of irrigation, the one canal deserves special mention, as showing how George Stephenson came to Jodhpur and astonished the inhabitants. Six miles from the city proper lies the Balsaman Sagar, a great tank. In the hot weather, when the city tanks ran out or stank, it was the pleasant duty of the women to tramp twelve miles at the end of the day's work to fill their lotahs. In the hot weather Jodhpur is – let a simile suffice. Sukkur in June would be Simla to Jodhpur.

The State Engineer, who is also the Jodhpur State Line, for he has no European subordinates, conceived the idea of bringing the water from the Balsaman into the city. Was the city grateful? Not in the least. It is said that the Sahib wanted the water to run uphill and was throwing money into the tank. Being true Marwaris, men betted on the subject. The canal – a built-out one, for water must not touch earth in these parts – was made at a cost of something over a lakh, and the water came down because its source was a trifle higher than the city. Now, in the hot weather, the women need not go for long walks, but the Marwari cannot understand how it was that the waters came down to Jodhpur. From the Marwari to money matters is an easy step. Formerly, that is to say, up to within a very short time, the Treasury of Jodhpur was conducted in a shiftless, happy-go-lucky sort of fashion, not uncommon in Native States, whereby the Mahajuns 'held the bag' and made unholy profits on discount and other things, to the confusion of the Durbar Funds and their own enrichment. There is now a Treasury modelled on English lines, and English in the important particular that money is not to be got from it for the asking, and the items of expenditure are strictly looked after.

In the middle of all this bustle of reform planned, achieved, frustrated, and replanned, and the never-ending underground warfare that surges in a Native State, move the English officers – the irreducible minimum of exiles. As a caste, the working Englishmen in Native States are curiously interesting; and the traveller whose tact by this time has been blunted by tramping, sits in judgement upon them as he has seen them. In the first place, they are, they must be, the fittest who have survived; for though, here and there, you shall find one chafing bitterly against the burden of his life in the wilderness, one to be pitied more than any chained beast, the bulk of the caste are honestly and unaffectedly fond of their work, fond of the country around them, and fond of the people they deal with. In each State their answer to a question is the same. The men with whom they are in contact are 'all right' when you know them, but you've got to 'know them first', as the music-hall song says. Their hands are full of work; so full that, when the incult wanderer said: 'What do you find to do?' they look upon him with contempt and amazement, exactly as the wanderer himself had once looked upon a Globetrotter, who had put to him the same impertinent query. And – but here the Englishman may be wrong – it seemed to him that in one respect their lives were a good deal more restful and concentrated than those of their brethren under the British Government. There was no talk of shiftings and transfers and promotions, stretching across a Province and a half, and no man said anything about Simla. To one who has hitherto believed that Simla is the hub of the Empire, it is disconcerting to hear: 'Oh, Simla! That's where you Bengalis go. We haven't anything to do with Simla down here.' And no more they have. Their talk and their interests run in the boundaries of the states they serve, and, most striking of all, the gossipy element seems to be cut altogether. It is a backwater of the river of Anglo-Indian life – or is it the main current, the broad stream that supplies the motive power, and is the other life only the noisy ripple on the surface? You who have lived, not merely looked at, both lives, decide. Much can be learnt from the talk of the caste, many curious, many amusing, and some startling things. One hears stories of men who take a poor, impoverished state as a man takes a wife, 'for better or worse', and, moved by some incomprehensible ideal of virtue, consecrate – that is not too big a word – consecrate their lives to that state in all single-heartedness and purity. Such men are few, but they exist today, and their names are great in lands where no Englishman travels. Again the listener hears tales of grizzled diplomats of Rajputana – Machiavellis who have hoisted a powerful intriguer with his own intrigue, and bested priestly cunning, and the guile of the Oswal, simply that the way might be clear for some scheme which should put money into a tottering Treasury, or lighten the taxation of a few hundred thousand men – or both; for this can be done. One tithe of that force spent on their own personal advancement would have carried such men very far.

Truly the Hat-marked Caste are a strange people. They are so few and so lonely and so strong. They can sit down in one place for years, and see the works of their hands and the promptings of their brain grow to actual and beneficent life, bringing good to thousands. Less fettered than the direct servant of the Indian Government, and working over a much vaster charge, they seem a bigger and a more large-minded breed. And that is saying a good deal.

But let the others, the little people bound down and supervised, and strictly limited and income-taxed, always remember that the Hat-marked are very badly off for shops. If they want a necktie they must get it up from Bombay, and in the rains they can hardly move about; and they have no amusements and must go a day's railway journey for a rubber, and their drinking-water is doubtful: and there is less than one white woman *per* ten thousand square miles.

After all, comparative civilisation has its advantages.

Part 2

Of freedom and the necessity of using her. The motive and the scheme that will come to nothing. A disquisition upon the otherness of things and the torments of the damned.

After seven years it pleased Necessity, whom we all serve, to turn to me and say: 'Now you need do Nothing Whatever. You are free to enjoy yourself. I will take the yoke of bondage from your neck for one year. What do you choose to do with my gift?' And I considered the matter in several lights. At first I held notions of regenerating Society; but it appeared that this would demand more than a year, and perhaps Society would not be grateful after all. Then I would fain enter upon one monumental 'bust'; but I reflected that this at the outside could endure but three months, while the headache would last for nine. Then came by the person that I most hate – a Globetrotter. He, sitting in my chair, discussed India with the unbridled arrogance of five weeks on a Cook's ticket. He was from England and had dropped his manners in the Suez Canal. 'I assure you,' said he, 'that you who live so close to the actual facts of things cannot form dispassionate judgements of their merits. You are too near. Now I –' he waved his hand modestly and left me to fill the gaps.

I considered him, from his new helmet to his deck-shoes, and I perceived that he was but an ordinary man. I thought of India, maligned and silent India, given up to the ill-considered wanderings of such as he – of the land whose people are too busy to reply to the libels upon their life and manners. It was my destiny to avenge India upon nothing less than three-quarters of the world. The idea necessitated sacrifices – painful sacrifices – for I had to become a Globetrotter, with a helmet and deck-shoes. In the interests of our little world I would endure these things and more. I would deliver 'brawling judgements all day long; on all things unashamed'. I would go toward the rising sun till I reached the heart of the world and once more smelt London asphalt.

The Indian public never gave me a brief. I took it, appointing myself Commissioner in General for Our Own Sweet Selves. Then all the aspects of life changed, as, they say, the appearance of his room grows strange to a dying man when he sees it upon the last morning, and knows that it will confront him no more. I had wilfully stepped aside from the current of our existence, and had no part in any of Our interests. Up-country the peach was beginning to bud, and men said that by cause of the heavy snows in the hills the hot weather would be a short one. That was nothing to me. The punkahs and their pullers sat together in the veranda, and the public buildings spawned thermantidotes. The copper-smith sang in the garden and the early wasp hummed low down by the door handle, and they prophesied of the hot weather to come. These things were no concern of mine. I was dead, and looked upon the old life as a dead man – without interest and without concern.

It was a strange life; I had lived it for seven years or one day, I could not be certain which. All that I knew was that I could watch men going to their offices, while I slept luxuriously; could go out at any hour of the day and sit up to any hour of the night, secure that each morning would bring no toil. I understood with what emotions the freed convict regards the prison he has quitted – insight which had hitherto been denied me; and I further saw how intense is the selfishness of the irresponsible man. Some said that the coming year would be one of scarcity and distress because unseasonable rains were falling. I was grieved. I feared that the Rains might break the railway line to the sea, and so delay my departure. Again, the season would be a sickly one. I fancied that Necessity might repent of her gift and for mere jest wipe me off the face of the earth ere I had seen anything of what lay upon it. There was trouble on the Afghan frontier; perhaps an army-corps would be mobilised, and perhaps many men would die, leaving folk to mourn for them at the hill stations. My dread was that a Russian man-of-war might intercept the steamer which carried my precious self between Yokohama and San Francisco. Let Armageddon be postponed, I prayed, for my sake, that my personal enjoyments may not be interfered with. War, famine, and pestilence would be so inconvenient to me. And I abased myself before Necessity, the great Goddess, and said ostentatiously: 'It is naught, it is naught, and you needn't look at me when I wander about.' Surely we are only virtuous by compulsion of earning our daily bread.

So I looked upon men with new eyes, and pitied them very much indeed. They worked. They had to. I was an aristocrat. I could call upon them at inconvenient hours and ask them why they worked, and whether they did it often. Then they grunted, and the envy in their eyes was a delight to me. I dared not, however, mock them too pointedly, lest Necessity should drag me back by the collar to take my still warm place by their side. When I had disgusted all who knew me, I fled to Calcutta, which, I was pained to see, still persisted in being a city and transacting commerce after I had formally cursed it one year ago. That curse I now repeat, in the hope that the unsavoury capital will collapse. One must begin to smoke at five in the morning – which is neither night nor day – on coming across the Howrah Bridge, for it is better to get a headache from honest nicotine than to be poisoned by evil smells. And a man, who otherwise was a nice man, though he worked with his hands and his head, asked me why the scandal of the Simla Exodus was allowed to continue. To him I made answer: 'It is because this sewer is unfit for human habitation. It is because you are all one gigantic mistake – you and your monuments and your merchants and everything about you. I rejoice to think that scores of lakhs of rupees have been spent on public offices at a place called Simla, that scores and scores will be spent on the Delhi-Kalka line, in order that civilised people may go there in comfort. When that line is opened, your big city will be dead and buried and done with, and I hope it will teach you a lesson. Your city will rot, Sir.' And he said: 'When people are buried here, they turn into adipocere in five days if the weather is rainy. They saponify, you know.' I said: 'Go and saponify, for I hate Calcutta.' But he took me to the Eden Gardens instead, and begged me for my own sake not to go round the world in this prejudiced spirit. I was unhappy and ill, but he vowed that my spleen was due to my 'Simla way of looking at things'.

All this world of ours knows something about the Eden Gardens, which are supposed by the uninitiated of the mofussil to represent the gilded luxury of the metropolis. As a matter of fact they are hideously dull. The inhabitants appear in top-hats and frock-coats, and walk dolorously to and fro under the glare of jerking electric lamps, when they ought to be sitting in their shirt-sleeves round little tables and treating their wives to iced lager beer. My friend – it was a muggy March night – wrapped himself in the prescribed garments and said graciously: 'You can wear a round hat, but you mustn't wear deck-shoes; and for goodness' sake, my dear fellow, don't smoke on the Red Road – all the people one knows go there.' Most of the people who were people sat in their carriages, in an atmosphere of hot horse, harness, and panel-lacquer, outside the gardens, and the remnant tramped up anddown, by twos and threes, upon squashy green grass, until they were wearied, while a band played at them. 'And is this all you do?' I asked. 'It is,' said my friend. 'Isn't it good enough? We meet everyone we know here, and walk with him or her, unless he or she is among the carriages.'

Overhead was a woolly warm sky; underfoot feverish soft grass; and from all quarters the languorous breeze bore faint reminiscences of stale sewage upon its wings. Round the horizon were stacked lines of carriages, and the electric flare bred aches in the strained eyebrow. It was a strange sight and fascinating. The doomed creatures walked up and down without cessation, for when one fled away into the lamp-spangled gloom twenty came to take his place. Slop-hatted members of the mercantile marine, Armenian merchants, Bengal civilians, shop-girls and shop-men, Jews, Parthians, and Mesopotamians, were all there in the tepid heat and the fetid smell.

'This,' said my friend, 'is how we enjoy ourselves. There are the Viceregal liveries. Lady Lansdowne comes here.' He spoke as though reading to me the Government House list of Paradise. I reflected that these people would continue to walk up and down until they died, drinkless, dusty, sad, and blanched.

In saying this last thing I had made a mistake. Calcutta is no more Anglo-Indian than West Brompton. In common with Bombay, it has achieved a mental attitude several decades in advance of that of the raw and brutal India of fact. An intelligent and responsible financier, discussing the Empire, said: 'But why do we want so large an army in India? Look at the country all about.' I think he meant as far as the Circular Road or perhaps Raneegunge. Some of these days, when the voice of the two uncomprehending cities carries to London, and its advice is acted upon, there will be trouble. Till this second journey to Calcutta I was unable to account for the acid tone and limited range of the presidency journals. I see now that they are ward papers and ought to be treated as such.

In the fullness of time – there was no hurry – imagine that, O you toilers of the land – I took ship and fled from Calcutta by that which they call the Mutton-Mail, because it takes sheep and correspondence to Rangoon. Half the Punjab was going with us to serve the Queen in the Burma Military Police, and it was grateful to catch once more the raw, rasping up-country speech amid the jabber of Burmese and Bengali.

To Rangoon, then, aboard the *Madura*, come with me down the Hughli, and try to understand what sort of life is led by the pilots, those strange men who only seem to know the land by watching it from the river.

'And I fetched up under the north ridge with six inches o' water under me, with a sou'west monsoon blowing, an' me not knowing any more than the dead where in – Paradise – I was taking her,' says one deep voice.

'Well, what do you expect?' says another. 'They ought not all to be occulting lights. Give me a red with two flashes for outlying danger anyhow. The Hughli's the worst river in the world. Why, off the Lower Gasper only last year…'

'And look at the way Government treats you!'

The Hughli pilot is human. He may talk Greek in the exercise of his profession, but he can unite at swearing at the Government as thoroughly as though he were an uncovenanted civilian. His life is a hard one; but he is full of strange stories, and when treated with proper respect may condescend to tell some of them. If he has served on the river for six years as a 'cub' and is neither dead nor decrepit, I believe he can earn as much as fifty rupees by sending two thousand tons of ship and a few hundred souls flying down the reaches at twelve miles an hour. Then he drops over the side with your last love-letters and wanders about the estuary in a tug until he finds another steamer and brings her up. It does not take much to comfort him.

Somewhere in the open sea some days later. I give it up. I *cannot* write, and to sleep I am not ashamed. A glorious idleness has taken entire possession of me; journalism is an imposture; so is Literature; so is Art. All India dropped out of sight yesterday and the rocking pilot-brig at the Sandheads bore my last message to the prison that I quit. We have reached blue water – crushed sapphire – and a little breeze is bellying the awning. Three flying-fish were sighted this morning; the tea at *chota-hazri* is not nice, but the captain is excellent. Is this budget of news sufficiently exciting, or must I in strict confidence tell you the story of the Professor and the compass? You will hear more about the Professor later, if, indeed, I ever touch pen again. When he was in India he worked about nine hours a day. At noon today he conceived an interest in cyclones and things of that kind – would go to his cabin to get a compass and a meteorological book. He went, but stopped to reflect by the brink of a drink. 'The compass is in a box,' said he, drowsily, 'but the nuisance of it is that to get it I shall have to pull the box out from under my berth. All things considered, I don't think it's worthwhile.' He loafed on deck, and I think by this time is fast asleep. There was no trace of shame in his voice for his mighty sloth. I would have reproved him, but the words died on my tongue. I was guiltier than he.

'Professor,' said I, 'there is a foolish little paper in Allahabad called the *Pioneer*. I am supposed to be writing it a letter – a letter with my hands! Did you ever hear of anything so absurd?'

'I wonder if Angostura bitters really go with whisky,' said the Professor, toying with the neck of the bottle.

There is no such place as India; there never was a daily paper called the *Pioneer*. It was all a weary dream. The only real things in the world are crystal seas, clean-swept decks, soft rugs, warm sunshine, the smell of salt in the air, and fathomless, futile indolence.

Burma

The river of the lost footsteps and the golden mystery upon its banks. The iniquity of Jordan. Shows how a man may go to the Shway Dagon pagoda and see it not.

There was a river and a bar, a pilot and a great deal of nautical mystery, and the Captain said the journey from Calcutta was ended and that we should be in Rangoon in a few hours. It is not an impressive stream, being low-banked, scrubby, and muddy; but as we gave the staggering rice-boats the go-by, I reflected that I was looking upon the River of the Lost Footsteps – the road that so many, many men of my acquaintance had travelled, never to return, within the past three years. Such a one had gone up to open out Upper Burma, and had himself been opened out by a Burmese dah in the cruel scrub beyond Minhla; such another had gone to rule the land in the Queen's name, but could not rule a hill stream and was carried down under his horse. One had been shot by his servant; another by a dacoit while he sat at dinner; and a pitifully long list had found in jungle-fever their sole reward for 'the difficulties and privations inseparably connected with military service', as the Bengal Army Regulations put it. I ran over half a score of names – policemen, subalterns, young civilians, employees of big trading firms, and adventurers. They had gone up the river and they had died. At my elbow stood one of the workers in New Burma, going to report himself at Rangoon, and he told tales of interminable chases after evasive dacoits, of marchings and countermarchings that came to nothing, and of deaths in the wilderness as noble as they were sad.

Then, a golden mystery upheaved itself on the horizon – a beautiful winking wonder that blazed in the sun, of a shape that was neither Muslim dome nor Hindu temple spire. It stood upon a green knoll, and below it were lines of warehouses, sheds, and mills. Under what new god, thought I, are we irrepressible English sitting now?

'There's the old Shway Dagon' (pronounced Dagone, *not* like the god in the Scriptures), said my companion. 'Confound it!' But it was not a thing to be sworn at. It explained in the first place why we took Rangoon, and in the second why we pushed on to see what more of rich or rare the land held. Up till that sight my uninstructed eyes could not see that the land differed much in appearance from the Sundarbans, but the golden dome said: 'This is Burma, and it will be quite unlike any land you know about.' 'It's a famous old shrine o' sorts,' said my companion, 'and now the Tounghoo-Mandalay line is open, pilgrims are flocking down by the thousand to see it. It lost its big gold top – thing that they call a *'htee* – in an earthquake: that's why it's all hidden by bamboo-work for a third of its height. You should see it when it's all uncovered. They're regilding it now.'

Why is it that when one views for the first time any of the wonders of the earth a bystander always strikes in with, 'You should see it, etc.'? Such men given twenty minutes from the tomb at the Day of Judgement, would patronize the naked souls as they hurried up with the glare of Tophet on their faces, and say: 'You should have seen this when Gabriel first began to blow.' What the Shway Dagon really is and how many books may have been written upon its history and archaeology is no part of my business. As it stood overlooking everything it seemed to explain all about Burma – why the boys had gone north and died, why the troopers bustled to and fro, and why the steamers of the Irrawaddy Flotilla lay like black-backed gulls upon the water.

Then we came to a new land, and the first thing that one of the regular residents said was: 'This place isn't India at all. They ought to have made it a Crown colony.' Judging the Empire as it ought to be judged, by its most prominent points – *videlicet*, its smells – he was right; for though there is one stink in Calcutta, another in Bombay, and a third and most pungent one in the Punjab, yet they have a kinship of stinks, whereas Burma smells quite otherwise. It is not exactly what China ought to smell like, but it is not India. 'What is it?' I asked; and the man said '*Napi*', which is fish pickled when it ought to have been buried long ago. This food, in guidebook language, is inordinately consumed by... but everybody who has been within downwind range of Rangoon knows what *napi* means, and those who do not will not understand.

Yes, it was a very new land – a land where the people understood colour – a delightfully lazy land full of pretty girls and very bad cheroots.

The worst of it was that the Anglo-Indian was a foreigner, a creature of no account. He did not know Burman – which was no great loss – and the Madrassi insisted upon addressing him in English. The Madrassi, by the way, is a great institution. He takes the place of the Burman, who will not work, and in a few years returns to his native coast with rings on his fingers and bells on his toes. The consequences are obvious. The Madrassi demands, and receives, enormous wages, and gets to know that he is indispensable. The Burman exists beautifully, while his womenfolk marry the Madrassi and the Chinaman, because these support them in affluence. When the Burman wishes to work he gets a Madrassi to do it for him. How he finds the money to pay the Madrassi I was not informed, but all men were agreed in saying that under no circumstances will the Burman exert himself in the paths of honest industry. Now, if a bountiful Providence had clothed you in a purple, green, amber or puce petticoat, had thrown a rose-pink scarf-turban over your head, and had put you in a pleasant damp country where rice grew of itself and fish came up to be caught, putrified and pickled, would *you* work? Would you not rather take a cheroot and loaf about the streets seeing what was to be seen? If two-thirds of your girls were grinning, good-humoured little maidens and the remainder positively pretty, would you not spend your time in making love?

The Burman does both these things, and the Englishman, who after all worked himself to Burma, says hard things about him. Personally I love the Burman with the blind favouritism born of first impression. When I die I will be a Burman, with twenty yards of real King's silk, that has been made in Mandalay, about my body, and a succession of cigarettes between my lips. I will wave the cigarette to emphasise my conversation, which shall be full of jest and repartee, and I will always walk about with a pretty almond-coloured girl who shall laugh and jest too, as a young maiden ought. She shall not pull a sari over her head when a man looks at her and glare suggestively from behind it, nor shall she tramp behind me when I walk: for these are the customs of India. She shall look all the world between the eyes, in honesty and good fellowship, and I will teach her not to defile her pretty mouth with chopped tobacco in a cabbage leaf, but to inhale good cigarettes of Egypt's best brand.

Seriously, the Burmese girls are very pretty, and when I saw them I understood much that I had heard about – about our army in Flanders let us say.

Providence really helps those who do not help themselves. I went up a street, name unknown, attracted by the colour that was so wantonly flashed down its length. There is colour in Rajputana and in Southern India, and you can find a whole paletteful of raw tints at any down-country durbar; but the Burmese way of colouring is different. With the women the scarf, petticoat, and jacket are of three lively hues, and with the men putso and head-wrap are gorgeous. Thus you get your colours dashed down in dots against a background of dark timber houses set in green foliage. There are no canons of art anywhere, and every scheme of colouring depends on the power of the sun above. That is why men in a London fog do still believe in pale greens and sad reds. Give me lilac, pink, vermilion, lapis lazuli, and blistering blood red under fierce sunlight that mellows and modifies all. I had just made this discovery and was noting that the people treated their cattle kindly, when the driver of an absurd little hired carriage built to the scale of a fat Burma pony, volunteered to take me for a drive, and we drove in the direction of the English quarter of the town where the sahibs live in dainty little houses made out of the sides of cigar boxes. They looked as if they could be kicked in at a blow and (trust a Globetrotter for evolving a theory at a minute's notice) it is to avoid this fate that they are built for the most part on legs. The houses are not cantonment bred in any way – nor did the uneven ground and dusty reddish roads fit in with any part of the Indian Empire except it may be Ootacamund.

The pony wandered into a garden studded with lovely little lakes which, again, were studded with islands, and there were sahibs in flannels in the boats. Outside the park were pleasant little monasteries full of clean-shaved gentlemen in gold amber robes learning to renounce the world, the flesh, and the devil by chatting furiously amongst themselves, and at every corner stood the three little maids from school, almost exactly as they had been dismissed from the side scenes of the Savoy after the *Mikado* was over: and the strange part of it all was that everyone laughed – laughed, so it seemed, at the sky above them because it was blue, at the sun because it was sinking, and at each other because they had nothing better to do. A small fat child laughed loudest of all, in spite of the fact that it was smoking a cheroot that ought to have made it deathly sick. The pagoda was always close at hand – as brilliant a mystery as when first sighted far down the river; but it changed its shape as we came nearer, and showed in the middle of a nest of hundreds of smaller pagodas. There appeared suddenly two colossal tigers (after the Burmese canons) in plaster on a hillside, and they were the guardians of Burma's greatest pagoda. Round them rustled a great crowd of happy people in pretty dresses, and the feet of all were turned towards a great stoneway that ran from between the tigers even to the brow of the mound. But the nature of the stairs was peculiar. They were covered in for the most part by a tunnel, or it may have been a walled-in colonnade, for there were heavily gilt wooden pillars visible in the gloom. The afternoon was drawing on as I came to this strange place and saw that I should have to climb up a long, low hill of stairs to get to the pagoda.

Once or twice in my life I have seen a Globetrotter literally gasping with jealous emotion because India was so much larger and more lovely than he had ever dreamed, and because he had only set aside three months to explore it in. My own sojourn in Rangoon was countable by hours, so I may be forgiven when I pranced with impatience at the bottom of the staircase because I could not at once secure a full, complete, and accurate idea of everything that was to be seen. The meaning of the guardian tigers, the inwardness of the main pagoda, and the countless little ones, was hidden from me. I could not understand why the pretty girls with cheroots sold little sticks and coloured candles to be used before the image of Buddha. Everything was incomprehensible to me, and there was none to explain. All that I could gather was that in a few days the great golden *'htee* that has been defaced by the earthquake would be hoisted into position with feasting and song, and that half Upper Burma was coming down to see the show.

I went forward between the two great beasts, across a whitewashed court, till I came to a flat-headed arch guarded by the lame, the blind, the leper, and the deformed. These plucked at my clothes as I passed, and moaned and whined: but the stream that disappeared up the gentle slope of the stairway took no notice of them. And I stepped into the semi-darkness of a long, long corridor flanked by booths, and floored with stones worn very smooth by human feet.

The city of elephants which is governed by the great god of idleness, who lives on the top of a hill. The history of three great discoveries.

So much for making definite programmes of travel beforehand. In my first letter I told you that I would go from Rangoon to Penang direct. Now we are lying off Moulmein in a new steamer which does not seem to run anywhere in particular. Why she should go to Moulmein is a mystery; but as every soul on the ship is a loafer like myself, no one is discontented. Imagine a shipload of people to whom time is no object, who have no desires beyond three meals a day and no emotions save those caused by a casual cockroach.

Moulmein is situated up the mouth of a river which ought to flow through South America, and all manner of dissolute native craft appear to make the place their home. Ugly cargo-steamers that the initiated call 'Geordie tramps' grunt and bellow at the beautiful hills all round, and the pot-bellied British India liners wallow down the reaches. Visitors are rare in Moulmein – so rare that few but cargo-boats think it worth their while to come off from the shore.

Strictly in confidence I will tell you that Moulmein is not a city of this earth at all. Sindbad the Sailor visited it, if you recollect, on that memorable voyage when he discovered the burial-ground of the elephants.

As the steamer came up the river we were aware of first one elephant and then another hard at work in timber yards that faced the shore. A few narrow-minded folk with binoculars said that there were *mahouts* upon their backs, but this was never clearly proven. I prefer to believe in what I saw – a sleepy town, just one house thick, scattered along a lovely stream and inhabited by slow, solemn elephants, building stockades for their own diversion. There was a strong scent of freshly sawn teak in the air – we could not see any elephants sawing – and occasionally the warm stillness was broken by the crash of the log. When the elephants had got an appetite for luncheon they loafed off in couples to their club, and did not take the trouble to give us greeting and the latest mail papers; at which we were much disappointed, but took heart when we saw upon a hill a large white pagoda surrounded by scores of little pagodas. 'This,' we said with one voice, 'is the place to make an excursion to,' and then shuddered at our own profanity, for above all things we did not wish to behave like mere vulgar tourists.

The *ticca-gharies* at Moulmein are three sizes smaller than those of Rangoon, as the ponies are no bigger than decent sheep. Their drivers trot them uphill and down, and as the *ghari* is extremely narrow and the roads are anything but good, the exercise is refreshing. Here again all the drivers are Madrassis.

I should better remember what that pagoda was like had I not fallen deeply and irrevocably in love with a Burmese girl at the foot of the first flight of steps. Only the fact of the steamer starting next noon prevented me from staying at Moulmein for ever and owning a pair of elephants. These are so common that they wander about the streets, and, I make no doubt, could be obtained for a piece of sugarcane.

Leaving this far too lovely maiden, I went up the steps only a few yards, and, turning me round, looked upon a view of water, island, broad river, fair grazing ground, and belted wood that made me rejoice that I was alive. The hillside below me and above me was ablaze with pagodas – from a gorgeous golden and vermilion beauty to a delicate grey stone one just completed in honour of an eminent priest lately deceased at Mandalay. Far above my head there was a faint tinkle, as of golden bells, and a talking of the breezes in the tops of the toddy-palms. Wherefore I climbed higher and higher up the steps till I reached a place of great peace, dotted with Burmese images, spotlessly clean. Here women now and again paid reverence. They bowed their heads and their lips moved, because they were praying. I had an umbrella – a black one – in my hand, deck-shoes upon my feet, and a helmet upon my head. I did not pray – I swore at myself for being a Globetrotter, and wished that I had enough Burmese to explain to these ladies that I was sorry and would have taken off my hat but for the sun. A Globetrotter is a brute. I had the grace to blush as I tramped round the pagoda. That will be remembered to me for righteousness. But I stared horribly – at a gold and red side-temple with a beautifully gilt image of Buddha in it – at the grim figures in the niches at the base of the main pagoda – at the little palms that grew out of the cracks in the tiled paving of the court – at the big palms above, and at the low hung bronze bells that stood at each corner for the women to smite with stag-horns. Upon one bell rang this amazing triplet in English, evidently the composition of the caster, who completed his work – and now, let us hope, has reached Nibban – thirty-five years ago:

He who destroyed this Bell
They must be in the great Hel
And unable to coming out.

I respect a man who is not able to spell Hell properly. It shows that he has been brought up in an amiable creed. You who come to Moulmein treat this bell with respect, and refrain from playing with it, for that hurts the feelings of the worshippers.

In the base of the pagoda were four rooms, lined as to three sides with colossal plaster figures, before each of whom burned one solitary dip whose rays fought with the flood of evening sunshine that came through the windows, and the room was filled with a pale yellow light – unearthly to stand in. Occasionally a woman crept in to one of these rooms to pray, but nearly all the company stayed in the courtyard; but those that faced the figures prayed more zealously than the others, so I judged that their troubles were the greater. Of the actual cult I knew less than nothing; for the neatly bound English books that we read make no mention of pointing red-tipped straws at a golden image, or of the banging of bells after the custom of worshippers in a Hindu temple. It must be a genial one, however. To begin with, it is quiet and carried on among the fairest possible surroundings that ever landscape offered.

In this particular case, the massive white pagoda shot into the blue from the west of a walled hill that commanded four separate and desirable views as you looked either at the steamer in the river below, the polished silver reaches to the left, the woods to the right, or the roofs of Moulmein to the landward. Between each pause of the rustling of dresses and the low-toned talk of the women fell, from far above, the tinkle of innumerable metal leaves which were stirred by the breeze as they hung from the *'htee* of the pagoda. A golden image winked in the sun; the painted ones stared straight in front of them over the heads of the worshippers, and somewhere below a mallet and a plane were lazily helping to build yet another pagoda in honour of the Lord of the Earth.

Sitting in meditation while the Professor went round with a sacrilegious camera, to the vast terror of the Burmese youth, I made two notable discoveries and nearly went to sleep over them. The first was that the Lord of the Earth is idleness – thick slab idleness with a little religion stirred in to keep it sweet, and the second was that the shape of the pagoda came originally from a bulging toddy-palm trunk. There was one between me and the far-off sky line, and it exactly duplicated the outlines of a small grey stone building.

Yet a third discovery, and a much more important one, came to me later on. A dirty little imp of a boy ran by clothed more or less in a beautifully worked silk putso, the like of which I had in vain attempted to secure at Rangoon. A bystander told me that such an article would cost one hundred and ten rupees – exactly ten rupees in excess of the price demanded at Rangoon, when I had been discourteous to a pretty Burmese girl with diamonds in her ears, and had treated her as though she were a Delhi boxwallah.

'Professor,' said I, when the camera spidered round the corner, 'there is something wrong with this people. They won't work, they aren't all dacoits, and their babies run about with hundred-rupees putsoes on them, while their parents speak the truth. How in the world do they get a living?'

'They exist beautifully,' said the Professor; 'and I only brought half a dozen plates with me. I shall come again in the morning with some more. Did I ever dream of a place like this?'

'No,' said I. 'It's perfect, and for the life of me I can't quite see where the precise charm lies.'

'In its beastly laziness,' said the Professor, as he packed the camera, and we went away, regretfully, haunted by the voices of many wind-blown bells.

Not ten minutes from the pagoda we saw a real British bandstand, a shanty labelled 'Municipal Office', a collection of PWD bungalows that in vain strove to blast the landscape, and a Madras band. I had never seen Madrassi troops before. They seem to dress just like Tommies, and have an air of much culture and refinement. It is said that they read English books and know all about their rights and privileges. For further details apply to the Pegu Club, second table from the top on the right hand side as you enter.

In an evil hour I attempted to revive the drooping trade of Moulmein, and to this end bound a native of the place to come on board the steamer next morn with a collection of Burmese silks. It was only a five minutes' pull, and he could have sat in the stern all the while. Morning came, but not the man. Not a boat of watermelons, pink fleshy watermelons, neared the ship. We might have been in quarantine. As we slipped down the river on our way to Penang, I saw the elephants playing with the teak logs as solemnly and as mysteriously as ever. They were the chief inhabitants, and, for aught I know, the rulers of the place. Their lethargy had corrupted the town, and when the Professor wished to photograph them, I believe they went away in scorn.

Penang

Showing how I came to Palmiste Island and the place of Paul and Virginia, and fell asleep in a garden. A disquisition on the folly of sightseeing.

There is something very wrong in the Anglo-Saxon character. Hardly had the *Africa* dropped anchor in Penang Straits when two of our fellow passengers were smitten with madness because they heard that another steamer was even then starting for Singapore. If they went by it they would gain several days. Heaven knows why time should have been so precious to them. The news sent them flying into their cabins, and packing their trunks as though their salvation depended upon it. Then they tumbled over the side and were rowed away in a sampan, hot, but happy. They were on a pleasure-trip, and they had gained perhaps three days. That was their pleasure.

Do you recollect Besant's description of Palmiste Island in *My Little Girl* and *So They Were Married*? Penang is Palmiste Island. I found this out from the ship, looking at the wooded hills that dominate the town, and at the regiments of palm trees three miles away that marked the coast of Wellesley Province. The air was soft and heavy with laziness, and at the ship's side were boat-loads of much jewelled Madrassis – even those to whom Besant has alluded. A squall swept across the water and blotted out the rows of low, red-tiled houses that made up Penang, and the shadows of night followed the storm.

I put my twelve-inch rule in my pocket to measure all the world by, and nearly wept with emotion when on landing at the jetty I fell against a Sikh – a beautiful bearded Sikh, with white leggings and a rifle. As is cold water in a thirsty land so is a face from the old country. My friend had come from Jandiala in the Umritsar district. Did I know Jandiala? Did I not? I began to tell all the news I could recollect about crops and armies and the movements of big men in the far, far north while the Sikh beamed. He belonged to the military police, and it was a good service, but of course it was far from the old country. There was no hard work, and the Chinamen gave but little trouble. They had fights among themselves, but 'they do not care to give *us* any impudence'; and the big man swaggered off with the long roll and swing of a whole Pioneer regiment, while I cheered myself with the thought that India – the India I pretend to hold in hatred – was not so far off, after all.

You know our ineradicable tendency to damn everything in the mofussil. Calcutta professes astonishment that Allahabad has a good dancing floor; Allahabad wonders if it is true that Lahore really has an ice-factory; and Lahore pretends to believe that everybody in Peshawar sleeps armed. Very much in the same way I was amused at seeing a steam tramway in Rangoon, and after we had quitted Moulmein fully expected to find the outskirts of civilisation. Vanity and ignorance were severely shocked when they confronted a long street of business – a street of two-storied houses, full of *ticca-gharies*, shop signs, and above all *jinrickshaws*.

You in India have never seen a proper rickshaw. There are about two thousand of them in Penang, and no two seem alike. They are lacquered with bold figures of dragons and horses and birds and butterflies: their shafts are of black wood bound with white metal, and so strong that the coolie sits upon them when he waits for his fare. There is only one coolie, but he is strong, and he runs just as well as six bell-men. He ties up his pigtail – being a Cantonese – and this is a disadvantage to sahibs who cannot speak Tamil, Malay, or Cantonese. Otherwise he might be steered like a camel.

The rickshaw men are patient and long-suffering. The evil-visaged person who drove my carriage lashed at them when they came within whip range, and did his best to drive over them as he headed for the waterfalls, which are five miles away from Penang Town. I expected that the buildings should stop, choked out among the dense growth of coconut. But they continued for many streets, very like Park and Middleton streets in Calcutta, where shuttered houses, which were half-bred between an Indian bungalow and a Rangoon rabbit-hutch, fought with the greenery and crotons as big as small trees. Now and again there blazed the front of a Chinese house, all open-work vermilion, lamp-black, and gold, with six-foot Chinese lanterns over the doorways and glimpses of quaintly cut shrubs in the well-kept gardens beyond.

We struck into roads fringed with native houses on piles, shadowed by the everlasting coconut palms heavy with young nuts. The heat was heavy with the smell of vegetation, and it was not the smell of the earth after the rains. Some bird-thing called out from the deeps of the foliage, and there was a mutter of thunder in the hills which we were approaching: but all the rest was very still – and the sweat ran down our faces in drops.

'Now you've got to walk up that hill,' said the driver, pointing to a small barrier outside a well-kept botanical garden; 'all the carriages stop here.' One's limbs moved as though leaden, and the breath came heavily, drawing in each time the vapour of a Turkish bath. The soil was alive with wet and warmth, and the unknown trees – I was too sleepy to read the labels that some offensively energetic man has written – were wet and warm too. Up on the hillside the voice of the water was saying something, but I was too sleepy to listen; and on the top of the hill lay a fat cloud just like an eiderdown quilt tucking everything in safely.

And in the afternoon they came unto a land
In which it seemed always afternoon.

I sat down where I was, for I saw that the upward path was very steep and was cut into rude steps, and an exposition of sleep had come upon me. I was at the mouth of a tiny gorge, exactly where the lotus-eaters had sat down when they began their song, for I recognised the waterfall and the air round my ears 'breathing as one that has a weary dream'.

I looked and beheld that I could not give in words the genius of the place. 'I can't play the flute, but I have a cousin who plays the violin.' I knew a man who could. Some people said he was not a nice man, and I might run the risk of contaminating morals, but nothing mattered in such a climate. See now, go to the very worst of Zola's novels and read there his description of a conservatory. That was it. Several months passed away, but there was neither chill nor burning heat to mark the passage of time. Only, with a sense of acute pain I felt that I must 'do' the waterfall, and I climbed up the steps in the hillside, though every boulder cried 'sit down', until I found a small stream of water coursing down the face of a rock, and a much bigger one down my own.

Then we went away to breakfast, the stomach being always more worthy than any amount of sentiment. A turn in the road hid the gardens and stopped the noise of the waters, and that experience was over for all time. Experiences are very like cheroots. They generally begin badly, taste perfect halfway through, and at the butt-end are things to be thrown away and never picked up again...

His name was John, and he had a pigtail five feet long – all real hair and no silk braided, and he kept an hotel by the way and fed us with a chicken, into whose innocent flesh onions and strange vegetables had been forced. Till then we had feared Chinamen, especially when they brought food, but now we will eat anything at their hands. The conclusion of the meal was a half-guinea pineapple and a siesta. This is a beautiful thing which we of India – but I am of India no more – do not understand. You lie down and wait for time to pass. You are not in the least wearied – and you would not go to sleep. You are filled with a divine drowsiness – quite different from the heavy sodden slumber of a hot-weather Sunday, or the businesslike repose of a Europe morning. Now I begin to despise novelists who write about *siestas* in cold climates. I know what the real thing means.

I want to go Home! I want to go back to India! I am miserable. The steamship *Nawab* at this time of the year ought to have been empty, instead of which we have one hundred first-class passengers and sixty-six second. All the pretty girls are in the latter class. Something must have happened at Colombo – two steamers must have clashed. We have the results of the collision, and we are a menagerie. The captain says that there ought to have been only ten or twelve passengers by rights, and had the rush been anticipated, a larger steamer would have been provided. Personally, I consider that half our shipmates ought to be thrown overboard. They are only travelling round the world for pleasure, and that sort of dissipation leads to the forming of hasty and intemperate opinions. Anyhow, give me freedom and the cockroaches of the British India, where we dined on deck, altered the hours of the meals by plebiscite, and were lords of all we saw. You know the chain-gang regulations of the P&O: how you must approach the captain standing on your head with your feet waving reverently; how you must crawl into the presence of the chief steward on your belly and call him Thrice-Puissant Bottle-washer; how you must not smoke abaft the sheep-pens; must not stand in the companion; must put on a clean coat when the ship's library is opened; and crowning injustice, must order your drinks for tiffin and dinner one meal in advance? How can a man full of Pilsener beer reach that keen-set state of quiescence needful for ordering his dinner liquor? This shows ignorance of human nature. The P&O want healthy competition. They call their captains commanders and act as though 'twere a favour to allow you to embark. Again, freedom and the British India for ever, and down with the comforts of a coolie ship and the prices of a palace!

There are about thirty women on board, and I have been watching with a certain amount of indignation their concerted attempt at killing the stewardess – a delicate and sweet-mannered lady. I think they will accomplish their end. The saloon is ninety feet long, and the stewardess runs up and down it for nine hours a day. In her intervals of relaxation she carries cups of beef-tea to the frail sylphs who cannot exist without food between 9 a.m. and 1 p.m. This morning she advanced to me and said, as though it were the most natural thing in the world: 'Shall I take away your teacup, sir?' She was a real white woman, and the saloon was full of hulking, half-bred Portuguese. One young Englishman let her take his cup, and actually did not turn round when he handed it. This is awful, and teaches me, as nothing else has done, how far I am from the blessed East. She (the stewardess) talks standing up, to men who sit down!

We in India are currently supposed to be unkind to our servants. I should very much like to see a sweeper doing one-half of the work these strapping white matrons and maids exact from their sister. They make her carry things about and don't even say, 'Thank you.' She has no name, and if you bawl, 'Stewardess,' she is bound to come. Isn't it degrading?

But the real reason of my wish to return is because I have met a lump of Chicago Jews and am afraid that I shall meet many more. The ship is full of Americans, but the American-German-Jew boy is the most awful of all. One of them has money, and wanders from bow to stern asking strangers to drink, bossing lotteries on the run, and committing other atrocities. It is currently reported that he is dying. Unfortunately he does not die quickly enough.

But the real monstrosity of the ship is an American who is not quite grown up. I cannot call it a boy, though officially it is only eight, wears a striped jacket, and eats with the children. It has the wearied appearance of an infant monkey – there are lines round its mouth and under its eyebrows. When it has nothing else to do it will answer to the name of Albert. It has been two years on the continuous travel; has spent a month in India; has seen Constantinople, Tripoli, Spain; has lived in tents and on horseback for thirty days and thirty nights, as it was careful to inform me; and has exhausted the round of this world's delights.

There is no flesh on its bones, and it lives in the smoking-room financing the arrangements of the daily lottery. I was afraid of it, but it followed me, and in a level expressionless voice began to tell me how lotteries were constructed. When I protested that I knew, it continued without regarding the interruption, and finally, as a reward for my patience, volunteered to give me the names and idiosyncrasies of all on board. Then it vanished through the smoking-room window because the door was only eight feet high, and therefore too narrow for that bulk of abnormal experiences. On certain subjects it was partly better informed than I; on others it displayed the infinite credulity of a two-year-old. But the wearied eyes were ever the same. They will be the same when it is fifty. I was more sorry for it than I could say. All its reminiscences had got jumbled, and incidents of Spain were baled into Turkey and India. Some day a schoolmaster will get hold of it and try to educate it, and I should dearly like to see at which end he will begin. The head is too full already and the – the other part does not exist. Albert is, I presume, but an ordinary American child. He was to me a revelation. Now I want to see a little American girl – but not now – not just now. My nerves are shattered by the Jews and Albert; and unless they recover their tone I shall turn back at Yokohama.

Hong Kong

Shows how I arrived in China and saw entirely through the Great Wall and out upon the other side.

The past few days on the *Nawab* have been spent amid a new people and a very strange one. There were speculators from South Africa; financiers from home (these never talked in anything under hundreds of thousands of pounds and, I fear, bluffed awfully); there were consuls of far-off China ports and partners of China shipping houses talking a talk and thinking thoughts as different from Ours as is Our slang from the slang of London. But it would not interest you to learn the story of our shipload – to hear about the hard-headed Scotch merchant with a taste for spiritualism, who begged me to tell him whether there was really anything in theosophy and whether Tibet was full of levitating *chelas*, as he believed; or of the little London curate out for a holiday who had seen India and had faith in the progress of missionary work there – who believed that the CMS was shaking the thoughts and convictions of the masses, and that the Word of the Lord would ere long prevail above all other councils. He in the night-watches tackled and disposed of the great mysteries of Life and Death, and was looking forward to a lifetime of toil amid a parish without a single rich man in it.

When you are in the China Seas be careful to keep all your flannel-wear to hand. In an hour the steamer swung from tropical heat (including prickly) to a cold raw fog, as wet as a Scotch mist. Morning gave us a new world – somewhere between Heaven and Earth. The sea was smoked glass: reddish grey islands lay upon it under fog banks that hovered fifty feet above our heads. The squat sails of junks danced for an instant like autumn leaves in the breeze and disappeared, and there was no solidity in the islands against which the glassy levels splintered in snow. The steamer groaned and grunted and howled because she was so damp and miserable, and I groaned also because the guidebook said that Hong Kong had the finest harbour in the world, and I could not see two hundred yards in any direction. Yet this ghostlike in-gliding through the belted fog was livelily mysterious, and became more so when the movement of the air vouchsafed us a glimpse of a warehouse and a derrick, both apparently close aboard, and behind them the shoulder of a mountain. We made our way into a sea of flat-nosed boats all manned by most muscular humans, and the Professor said that the time to study the Chinese question was now. We, however, were carrying a new general to these parts, and nice, new, well-fitting uniforms came off to make him welcome; and in the contemplation of things too long withheld from me I forgot about the Pigtails. Gentlemen of the mess-room, who would wear linen coats on parade if you could, wait till you have been a month without seeing a patrol-jacket or hearing a spur go *ling-a-ling*, and you will know why civilians want you always to wear uniform. The General, by the way, was a nice General. He did not know much about the Indian Army or the ways of a gentleman called Roberts, if I recollect aright; but he said that Lord Wolseley was going to be Commander-in-Chief one of these days on account of the pressing needs of our Army. He was a revelation because he talked about nothing but English military matters, which are very, very different from Indian ones, and are mixed up with politics.

All Hong Kong is built on the sea face; the rest is fog. One muddy road runs for ever in front of a line of houses which are partly Chowringhee and partly Rotherhithe. You live in the houses, and when wearied of this, walk across the road and drop into the sea, if you can find a square foot of unencumbered water. So vast is the accumulation of country shipping, and such is its dirtiness as it rubs against the bund, that the superior inhabitants are compelled to hang their boats from davits above the common craft, who are greatly disturbed by a multitude of steam-launches. These ply for amusement and the pleasure of whistling, and are held in such small esteem that every hotel owns one, and the others are masterless. Beyond the launches lie more steamers than the eye can count, and four out of five of these belong to Us. I was proud when I saw the shipping at Singapore, but I swell with patriotism as I watch the fleets of Hong Kong from the balcony of the Victoria Hotel. I can almost spit into the water; but many mariners stand below and they are a strong breed.

How recklessly selfish does a traveller become! We had dropped for more than ten days all the world outside our trunks, and almost the first word in the hotel was: 'John Bright is dead, and there has been an awful hurricane at Samoa.'

'Ah! indeed that's very sad; but look here, where do you say my rooms are?' At home the news would have given talk for half a day. It was dismissed in half the length of a hotel corridor. One cannot sit down to think with a new world humming outside the window – with all China to enter upon and possess.

A rattling of trunks in the halls – a click of heels – and the apparition of an enormous gaunt woman wrestling with a small Madrassi servant... 'Yes – I haf travelled everywhere and I shall travel everywhere else. I go now to Shanghai and Pekin. I have been in Moldavia, Russia, Beirut, all Persia, Colombo, Delhi, Dacca, Benares, Allahabad, Peshawar, the Ali Musjid in that pass, Malabar, Singapore, Penang, here in this place, and Canton. I am Austrian-Croat, and I shall see the States of America and perhaps Ireland. I travel for ever; I am – how you call? – *veuve* – widow. My husband, he was dead; and so I am sad – I am always sad und so I trafel. I am alife of course, but I do not live. You onderstandt? Always sad. Vill you tell them the name of the ship to which they shall warf my trunks now. You trafel for pleasure? So! I trafel because I am alone und sad – always sad.'

The trunks disappeared, the door shut, the heels clicked down the passage, and I was left scratching my head in wonder. How did that conversation begin – why did it end, and what is the use of meeting eccentricities who never explained themselves? I shall never get an answer, but that conversation is true, every word of it. I see now where the fragmentary school of novelists get their material from.

When I went into the streets of Hong Kong I stepped into thick slushy London mud of the kind that strikes chilly through the boot, and the rattle of innumerable wheels was as the rattle of hansoms. A soaking rain fell, and all the sahibs hailed rickshaws – they call them ricks here – and the wind was chillier than the rain. It was the first touch of honest weather since Calcutta. No wonder with such a climate that Hong Kong was ten times livelier than Singapore, that there were signs of building everywhere, and gas-jets in all the houses, that colonnades and domes were scattered broadcast, and the Englishmen walked as Englishmen should – hurriedly and looking forward. All the length of the main street was veranda-ed, and the Europe shops squandered plate glass by the square yard. (*Nota bene* – As in Simla so elsewhere: mistrust the plate glass shops. You pay for their fittings in each purchase.)

The same Providence that runs big rivers so near to large cities puts main thoroughfares close to big hotels. I went down Queen Street, which is not very hilly. All the other streets that I looked up were built in steps after the fashion of Clovelly, and under blue skies would have given the Professor scores of good photographs. The rain and the fog blotted the views. Each upward-climbing street ran out in white mist that covered the sides of a hill, and the downward-sloping ones were lost in the steam from the waters of the harbour, and both were very strange to see. 'Hi-yi-yow,' said my rickshaw coolie and balanced me on one wheel. I got out and met first a German with a beard, then three jolly sailor boys from a man-of-war, then a sergeant of Sappers, then a Parsee, then two Arabs, then an American, then a Jew, then a few thousand Chinese all carrying something, and then the Professor.

'They make plates – instantaneous plates – in Tokyo, I'm told. What d'you think of that?' he said. 'Why, in India, the Survey

Department are the only people who make their own plates. Instantaneous plates in Tokyo; think of it!'

I had owed the Professor one for a long time. 'After all,' I replied, 'it strikes me that we have made the mistake of thinking too much of India. We thought we were civilised, for instance. Let us take a lower place. This beats Calcutta into a hamlet.'

And in good truth it did, because it was clean beyond the ordinary, because the houses were uniform, three storied, and veranda-ed, and the pavements were of stone. I met one horse, very ashamed of himself, who was looking after a cart on the sea road, but upstairs there are no vehicles save rickshaws. Hong Kong has killed the romance of the rickshaw in my mind. They ought to be sacred to pretty ladies, instead of which men go to office in them, officers in full canonicals use them; tars try to squeeze in two abreast, and from what I have heard down at the barracks they do occasionally bring to the guard-room the drunken defaulter. 'He falls asleep inside of it, Sir, and saves trouble.' The Chinese naturally have the town for their own, and profit by all our building improvements and regulations. Their golden and red signs flame down the Queen's Road, but they are careful to supplement their own tongue by well-executed Europe lettering. I found only one exception, thus:

Fussing, GarpenterAnd Gabinet Naktr
Has good GabiNets tor Sale.

The shops are made to catch the sailor and the curio hunter, and they succeed admirably. When you come to these parts put all your money in a bank and tell the manager man not to give it you, however much you ask. So shall you be saved from bankruptcy.

The Professor and I made a pilgrimage from Kee Sing even unto Yi King, who sells the decomposed fowl, and each shop was good. Though it sold shoes or sucking pigs, there was some delicacy of carving or gilded tracery in front to hold the eye, and each thing was quaint and striking of its kind. A fragment of twisted roots helped by a few strokes into the likeness of huddled devils, a running knop and flower cornice, a dull red and gold half-door, a split bamboo screen – they were all good, and their joinings and splicings and mortisings were accurate. The baskets of the coolies were good in shape, and the rattan fastenings that clenched them to the polished bamboo yoke were whipped down, so that there were no loose ends. You could slide in and out the drawers in the slung chests of the man who sold dinners to the rickshaw coolies; and the pistons of the little wooden hand-pumps in the shops worked accurately in their sockets.

Is there really such a place as Hong Kong? People say so, but I have not yet seen it. Once indeed the clouds lifted and I saw a granite house perched like a cherub on nothing, a thousand feet above the town. It looked as if it might be the beginning of a civil station, but a man came up the street and said, 'See this fog. It will be like this till September. You'd better go away.' I shall not go. I shall encamp in front of the place until the fog lifts and the rain ceases. At present, and it is the third day of April, I am sitting in front of a large coal fire and thinking of the 'frosty Caucasus' – you poor creatures in torment afar. And you think as you go to office and orderly-room that you are helping forward England's mission in the East. 'Tis a pretty delusion, and I am sorry to destroy it, but you have conquered the wrong country.

Let us annex China.

Some talk with a Taipan and a General; proves in what manner a sea picnic may be a success.

Hong Kong was so much alive, so built, so lighted, and so bloatedly rich to all outward appearance that I wanted to know how these things came about. You can't lavish granite by the cubic ton for nothing, or rivet your cliffs with Portland cement, or build a five-mile bund, or establish a club like a small palace. I sought a *Taipan*, which means the head of an English trading firm. He was the biggest *Taipan* on the island, and quite the nicest. He owned ships and wharves and houses and mines and a hundred other things. To him said:

'O *Taipan*, I am a poor person from Calcutta, and the liveliness of your place astounds me. How is it that everyone smells of money; whence come your municipal improvements; and why are the white men so restless?'

Said the *Taipan*: 'It is because the island is going ahead mightily. Because everything pays. Observe this share-list.'

He took me down a list of thirty or less companies – steam-launch companies, mining, rope-weaving, dock, trading, agency and general companies – and with five exceptions all the shares were at premium – some a hundred, some five hundred, and others only fifty.

'It is not a boom,' said the *Taipan*. 'It is genuine. Nearly every man you meet in these parts is a broker, and he floats companies.'

I looked out of the window and beheld how companies were floated. Three men with their hats on the back of their heads converse for ten minutes. To these enters a fourth with a pocket-book. Then all four dive into the Hong Kong Hotel for material wherewith to float themselves and – there is your company!

'From these things,' said the *Taipan*, 'comes the wealth of Hong Kong. Every notion here pays, from the dairy farm upwards. We have passed through our bad times and come to the fat years.'

He told me tales of the old times – pityingly because he knew I could not understand. All I could tell was that the place dressed by America – from the hair-cutters' saloons to the liquor-bars. The faces of men were turned to the Golden Gate even while they floated most of the Singapore companies. There is not sufficient push in Singapore alone, so Hong Kong helps. Circulars of new companies lay on the bank counters. I moved amid a maze of interests that I could not comprehend, and spoke to men whose minds were at Hankow, Foochoo, Amoy, or even further – beyond the Yangtze gorges where the Englishman trades.

After a while I escaped from the company-floaters because I knew I could not understand them, and ran up a hill. Hong Kong is all hill except when the fog shuts out everything except the sea. Tree ferns sprouted on the ground and azaleas mixed with the ferns, and there were bamboos over all. Consequently it was only natural that I should find a tramway that stood on its head and waved its feet in the mist. They called it the Victoria Gap Tramway and hauled it up with a rope. It ran up a hill into space at an angle of 65°, and to those who have seen the Rigi, Mount Washington, a switchback railway, and the like would not have been impressive. But neither you nor I have ever been hauled from Annandale to the Chaura Maidàn in a bee-line with a five-hundred-foot drop on the off-side, and we are at liberty to marvel. It is not proper to run up inclined ways at the tail of a string, more especially when you cannot see two yards in front of you and all earth below is a swirling cauldron of mist. Nor, unless you are warned of the opticalness of the delusion, is it nice to see from your seat, houses and trees at magic-lantern angles. Such things, before tiffin, are worse than the long roll of the China Seas.

They turned me out twelve hundred feet above the city on the military road to Dalhousie, as it will be when India has a surplus. Then they brought me a glorified dandy which, not knowing any better, they called a chair. Except that it is too long to run corners easily, a chair is vastly superior to a dandy. It is more like a Bombay side *tonjon* – the kind we use at Mahableshwar. You sit in a wicker chair, slung low on ten feet of elastic wooden shafting, and there are light blinds against the rain.

'We are now,' said the Professor, as he wrung out his hat gemmed with the dews of the driving mist, 'we are now on a pleasure trip. This is the road to Chakrata in the rains.'

'Nay,' said I; 'it is from Solon to Kasauli that we are going. Look at the black rocks.'

'Bosh!' said the Professor. 'This is a civilised country. Look at the road, look at the railings – look at the gutters.'

And as I hope never to go to Solon again, the road was cemented, the railings were of iron mortised into granite blocks, and the gutters were paved. 'Twas no wider than a hill-path, but if it had been the Viceroy's pet promenade it could not have been better kept. There was no view. That was why the Professor had taken his camera. We passed coolies widening the road, and houses shut up and deserted, solid squat little houses made of stone, with pretty names after our hill-station custom – Townend, Craggylands, and the like – and at these things my heart burned within me. Hong Kong has no right to mix itself up with Mussoorie in this fashion. We came to the meeting place of the winds, eighteen hundred feet above all the world, and saw forty miles of clouds. That was the Peak – the great view-place of the island. A laundry on a washing day would have been more interesting.

'Let us go down, Professor,' said I, 'and we'll get our money back. This isn't a view.'

We descended by the marvellous tramway, each pretending to be as little upset as the other, and started in pursuit of a Chinese burying-ground.

'Go to the Happy Valley,' said an expert. 'The Happy Valley, where the racecourse and the cemeteries are.'

'It's Mussoorie,' said the Professor. 'I knew it all along.'

It was Mussoorie, though we had to go through a half-mile of Portsmouth Hard first. Soldiers grinned at us from the verandas of their most solid three-storied barracks; all the blue-jackets of all the China squadron were congregated in the Royal Navy Seaman's Club, and they beamed upon us. The bluejacket is a beautiful creature, and very healthy, but... I gave my heart to Thomas Atkins long ago, and him I love.

By the way, how is it that a Highland regiment – the Argyll and Southerlandshire for instance – get such good recruits? Do the kilt and sporran bring in brawny youngsters of five-foot nine, and thirty-nine inch round the chest? The Navy draws well-built men also. How is it that Our infantry regiments fare so badly?

We came to the Happy Valley by way of a monument to certain dead Englishmen. Such things cease to move emotion after a little while. They are but the seed of the great harvest whereof our children's children shall assuredly reap the fruits. The men were killed in a fight, or by disease. We hold Hong Kong, and by Our strength and wisdom it is a great city, built upon a rock, and furnished with a dear little seven-furlong racecourse set in the hills, and fringed as to one side with the homes of the dead – Mahometan, Christian, and Parsee. A wall of bamboos shuts off the course and the grand-stand from the cemeteries. It may be good enough for Hong Kong, but would you care to watch your pony running with a grim reminder of 'gone to the drawer' not fifty feet behind you? Very beautiful are the cemeteries, and very carefully tended. The rocky hillside rises so near to them that the more recent dead can almost command a view of the racing as they lie. Even this far from the strife of the Churches they bury the different sects of Christians apart. One creed paints its wall white, and the other blue. The latter, as close to the race-stand as may be, writes in straggling letters, '*Hodie mihi cras tibi.*' No, I should *not* care to race in Hong Kong. The scornful assemblage behind the grand-stand would be enough to ruin any luck.

Chinamen do not approve of showing their cemeteries. We hunted ours from ledge to ledge of the hillsides, through crops and woods and crops again, till we came to a village of black and white pigs and riven red rocks beyond which the dead lay. It was a third-rate place, but was pretty. I have studied that oilskin mystery, the Chinaman, for at least five days, and why he should elect to be buried in good scenery, and by what means he knows good scenery when he sees it, I cannot fathom. But he gets it when the sight is taken from him, and his friends fire crackers above him in token of the triumph.

That night I dined with the *Taipan* in a palace. They say the merchant prince of Calcutta is dead – killed by exchange. Hong Kong ought to be able to supply one or two samples. The funny thing in the midst of all this wealth – wealth such as one reads about in novels – is to hear the curious deference that is paid to Calcutta. Console yourselves with that, gentlemen of the Ditch, for by my faith, it is the one thing that you can boast of. At this dinner I learned that Hong Kong was impregnable and that China was rapidly importing twelve and forty ton guns for the defence of her coasts. The one statement I doubted, but the other was truth. Those who have occasion to speak of China in these parts do so deferentially, as who should say: 'Germany intends such and such,' or 'These are the views of Russia.' The very men who talk thus are doing their best to force upon the great Empire all the stimulants of the West – railways, tram lines, and so forth. What will happen when China really wakes up, runs a line from Shanghai to Lhassa, starts another line of imperial Yellow Flag immigrant steamers, and really works and controls her own gun-factories and arsenals? The energetic Englishmen who ship the forty-tonners are helping to this end, but all they say is: 'We're well paid for what we do. There's no sentiment in business, and anyhow, China will never go to war with England.' Indeed, there is no sentiment in business. The *Taipan*'s palace, full of all things beautiful, and flowers more lovely than the gem-like cabinets they adorned, would have made happy half a hundred young men craving for luxury, and might have made them writers, singers and poets. It was inhabited by men with big heads and straight eyes, who sat among the splendours and talked business.

If I were not going to be a Burman when I die I would be a *Taipan* at Hong Kong. He knows so much and he deals so largely with princes and powers, and he has a flag of his very own which he pins on to all his steamers.

The blessed chance that looks after travellers sent me next day on a picnic, and all because I happened to wander into the wrong house. This is quite true, and very like our Anglo-Indian ways of doing things.

'Perhaps,' said the hostess, 'this will be our only fine day. Let us spend it in a steam-launch.'

Forthwith we embarked upon a new world – that of Hong Kong harbour – and with a dramatic regard for the fitness of things our little ship was the *Pioneer*. The picnic included the new General – he that came from England in the *Nawab* and told me about Lord Wolseley – and his aide-de-camp, who was quite English and altogether different from an Indian officer. He never once talked shop, and if he had a grievance hid it behind his moustache.

The harbour is a great world in itself. Photographs say that it is lovely, and this I can believe from the glimpses caught through the mist as the *Pioneer* worked her way between the lines of junks, the tethered liners, the wallowing coal hulks, the trim, low-lying American corvette, the *Orontes*, huge and ugly, the *Cockchafer*, almost as small as its namesake, the ancient three-decker converted into a military hospital – Thomas gets change of air thus – and a few hundred thousand sampans manned by women with babies tied on to their backs. Then we swept down the sea face of the city and saw that it was great, till we came to an unfinished fort high up on the side of a green hill, and I watched the new General as men watch an oracle. Have I told you that he is an Engineer General, specially sent out to attend to the fortifications? He looked at the raw earth and the granite masonry, and there was keen professional interest in his eye. Perhaps he would say something. I edged nearer in that hope. He did:

'Sherry and sandwiches? Thanks, I will. 'Stonishing how hungry the sea air makes a man feel,' quoth the General; and we went along under the grey-green coast, looking at stately country houses made of granite, where Jesuit fathers and opulent merchants dwell. It was the Mashobra of this Simla. It was also the Highlands, it was also Devonshire, and it was specially grey and chilly.

Never did *Pioneer* circulate in stranger waters. On the one side was a bewildering multiplicity of islets; on the other, the deeply indented shores of the main island, sometimes running down to the sea in little sandy coves, at others falling sheer in cliff and sea-worn cave full of the boom of the breakers. Behind, rose the hills into the mist, the everlasting mist.

'We are going to Aberdeen,' said the hostess; 'then to Stanley, and then across the island on foot by way of the Ti-tam reservoir. That will show you a lot of the country.'

We shot into a fjord and discovered a brown fishing village which kept sentry over two docks, and a Sikh policeman. All the inhabitants were rosy-cheeked women, each owning one-third of a boat, and a whole baby, wrapped up in red cloth and tied to the back. The mother was dressed in blue for a reason – if her husband whacked her over the shoulders, he would run a fair chance of crushing the baby's head unless the infant were of a distinct colour.

Then we left China altogether, and steamed into far Lochaber, with a climate to correspond. Good people under the punkah, think for a moment of cloud-veiled headlands running out into a steel-grey sea, crisped with a cheek-rasping breeze that makes you sit down under the bulwarks and gasp for breath. Think of the merry pitch and roll of a small craft as it buzzes from island to island, or venturously cuts across the mouth of a mile-wide bay, while you mature amid fresh scenery, fresh talk, and fresh faces, an appetite that shall uphold the credit of the great empire in a strange land. Once more we found a village which they called Stanley; but it was different from Aberdeen. Tenantless buildings of brownstone stared seaward from the low downs, and there lay behind them a stretch of weather-beaten wall. No need to ask what these things meant. They cried aloud: 'It is a deserted cantonment, and the population is in the cemetery.'

I asked, 'What regiment?'

'The Ninety-second, I think,' said the General. 'But that was in the old times – in the Sixties. I believe they quartered a lot of troops here and built the barracks on the ground; and the fever carried all the men off like flies. Isn't it a desolate place?'

My mind went back to a neglected graveyard a stone's throw from Jehangir's tomb in the gardens of Shalimar, where the cattle and the cowherd look after the last resting-places of the troops who first occupied Lahore. We are a great people and very strong, but we build Our empire in a wasteful manner – on the bones of the dead that have died of disease.

'But about the fortifications, General? Is it true that etc., etc.?'

'The fortifications are right enough as things go; what we want is men.'

'How many?'

'Say about three thousand for the Island – enough to stop any expedition that might come. Look at all these little bays and coves. There are twenty places at the back of the island where you could land men and make things unpleasant for Hong-Kong.'

'But,' I ventured, 'isn't it the theory that any organised expedition ought to be stopped by our fleet before it got here? Whereas the forts are supposed to prevent cutting out, shelling, and ransoming by a disconnected man-of-war or two.'

'If you go on that theory,' said the General, 'the men-of-war ought to be stopped by our fleets, too. That's all nonsense. If any power can throw troops here, you want troops to turn 'em out, and – don't we wish we may get them!'

'And you? Your command here is for five years, isn't it?'

'Oh, no! Eighteen months ought to see me out. I don't want to stick here for ever. I've other notions for myself,' said the General, scrambling over the boulders to get at his tiffin.

And that is just the worst of it. Here was a nice General helping to lay out fortifications, with one eye on Hong Kong and the other, his right one, on England. He would be more than human not to sell himself and his orders for the command of a brigade in the next English affair. He would be afraid of being too long away from home lest he should drop out of the running and... Well, we are just the same in India, and there is not the least hope of raising a Legion of the Lost for colonial service – of men who would do their work in one place for ever and look for nothing beyond it. But remember that Hong Kong – with five million tons of coal, five miles of shipping, docks, wharves, huge civil station, forty million pounds of trade, and the nicest picnic parties that you ever did see – wants three thousand men and – she won't get them. She has two batteries of garrison artillery, a regiment, and a lot of gun lascars – about enough to prevent the guns from rusting on their carriages. There are three forts on an island – Stonecutter's Island – between Hong Kong and the mainland, three on Hong Kong itself, and three or four scattered about elsewhere. Naturally the full complement of guns has not arrived. Even in India you cannot man forts without trained gunners. But tiffin under the lee of a rock was more interesting than colonial defence. A man cannot talk politics if he be empty.

Our one fine day shut in upon the empty plates in wind and rain, and the march across the island began.

As the launch was blotted out in the haze we squelched past sugarcane crops and fat pigs, past the bleak cemetery of dead soldiers on the hill, across a section of moor, till we struck a hill-road above the sea. The views shifted and changed like a kaleidoscope. First a shaggy shoulder of land tufted with dripping rushes and naught above, beneath, or around but mist and the straight spikes of the rain; then red road swept by water that fell into the unknown; then a combe, straight walled almost as a house, at the bottom of which crawled the jade-green sea; then a vista of a bay, a bank of white sand, and a red-sailed junk beating out before the squall; then only wet rock and fern, and the voice of thunder calling from peak to peak.

A landward turn in the road brought us to the pine woods of Theog and the rhododendrons – but they called them azaleas – of Simla, and ever the rain fell as though it had been July in the hills instead of April at Hong Kong. An invading army marching upon Victoria would have a sad time of it even if the rain did not fall. There are but one or two gaps in the hills through which it could travel, and there is a scheme in preparation whereby they shall be cut off and annihilated when they come. When I had to climb a clay hill backwards digging my heels into the dirt, I very much pitied that invading army.

Whether the granite-faced reservoir and two-mile tunnel that supplies Hong Kong with water be worth seeing I cannot tell. There was too much water in the air for comfort even when one tried to think of Home.

But go you and take the same walk – ten miles, and only two of 'em on level ground. Steam to the forsaken cantonment of Stanley and cross the island, and tell me whether you have seen anything so wild and wonderful in its way as the scenery. I am going up the river to Canton, and cannot stay for word-paintings.

Japan

Of Japan at ten hours' sight, containing a complete account of the manners and customs of its people, a history of its constitution, products, art, and civilisation, and omitting a meal in a teahouse with O-toyo.

This morning, after the sorrows of the rolling night, my cabin porthole showed me two great grey rocks studded and streaked with green and crowned by two stunted blue-black pines. Below the rocks a boat, that might have been carved sandalwood for colour and delicacy, was shaking out an ivory-white frilled sail to the wind of the morning. An indigo-blue boy with an old ivory face hauled on a rope. Rock and tree and boat made a panel from a Japanese screen, and I saw that the land was not a lie. This 'good brown earth' of ours has many pleasures to offer her children, but there be few in her gift comparable to the joy of touching a new country, a completely strange race, and manners contrary. Though libraries may have been written aforetime, each new beholder is to himself another Cortez. And I was in Japan – the Japan of cabinets and joinery, gracious folk and fair manners. Japan, whence the camphor and the lacquer and the shark-skin swords come: among what was it the books said? – a nation of artists. To be sure, we should only stop at Nagasaki for twelve hours ere going on to Kobé, but in twelve hours one can pack away a very fair collection of new experiences.

An execrable man met me on the deck, with a pale-blue pamphlet fifty pages thick. 'Have you,' said he, 'seen the Constitution of Japan? The Emperor made it himself only the other day. It is on entirely European lines.'

I took the pamphlet and found a complete paper Constitution stamped with the Imperial Chrysanthemum – an excellent little scheme of representation, reforms, payment of members, budget estimates, and legislation. It is a terrible thing to study at close quarters, because it is so pitifully English.

There was a yellow-shot greenness upon the hills round Nagasaki different, so my willing mind was disposed to believe, from the green of other lands. It was the green of a Japanese screen, and the pines were screen pines. The city itself hardly showed from the crowded harbour. It lay low among the hills, and its business face – a grimy bund – was sloppy and deserted. Business, I was rejoiced to learn, was at a low ebb in Nagasaki. The Japanese should have no concern with business. Close to one of the still wharves lay a ship of the Bad People; a Russian steamer down from Vladivostok. Her decks were cumbered with raffle of all kinds; her rigging was as frowsy and draggled as the hair of a lodging-house slavey, and her sides were filthy.

'That,' said a man of my people, 'is a very fair specimen of a Russian. You should see their men-of-war; they are just as filthy. Some of 'em come into Nagasaki to clean.'

It was a small piece of information and perhaps untrue, but it put the roof to my good humour as I stepped on to the bund and was told in faultless English by a young gentleman, with a plated chrysanthemum in his forage cap and badly fitting German uniform on his limbs, that he did not understand my language. He was a Japanese customs official. Had our stay been longer, I would have wept over him because he was a hybrid – partly French, partly German, and partly American – a tribute to civilisation. All the Japanese officials from police upwards seem to be clad in Europe clothes, and never do those clothes fit. I think the Mikado made them at the same time as the Constitution. They will come right in time.

When the rickshaw, drawn by a beautiful apple-cheeked young man with a Basque face, shot me into the *Mikado*, First Act, I did not stop and shout with delight, because the dignity of India was in my keeping. I lay back on the velvet cushions and grinned luxuriously at Pittising, with her sash and three giant hairpins in her blue-black hair, and three-inch clogs on her feet.

She laughed – even as did the Burmese girl in the old Pagoda at Moulmein. And her laugh, the laugh of a lady, was my welcome to Japan. Can the people help laughing? I think not. You see they have such thousands of children in their streets that the elders must perforce be young lest the babes should grieve. Nagasaki is inhabited entirely by children. The grown-ups exist on sufferance. A four-foot child walks with a three-foot child, who is holding the hand of a two-foot child, who carries on her back a one-foot child, who – but you will not believe me if I say that the scale runs down to six-inch little Japanese dolls such as they used to sell in the Burlington Arcade. These dolls wriggle and laugh. They are tied up in a blue bed-gown which is tied by a sash, which again ties up the bed-gown of the carrier. Thus if you untie that sash, baby and but little bigger brother are at once perfectly naked. I saw a mother do this, and it was for all the world like the peeling of hard-boiled eggs.

If you look for extravagance of colour, for flaming shop fronts and glaring lanterns, you shall find none of these things in the narrow stone-paved streets of Nagasaki. But if you desire details of house construction, glimpses of perfect cleanliness, rare taste, and perfect subordination of the thing made to the needs of the maker, you shall find all you seek and more. All the roofs are dull lead colour, being shingled or tiled, and all the house fronts are of the colour of the wood as God made it. There is neither smoke nor haze, and in the clear light of a clouded sky I could see down the narrowest alleyway as into the interior of a cabinet.

The books have long ago told you how a Japanese house is constructed, chiefly of sliding screens and paper partitions, and everybody knows the story of the burglar of Tokyo who burgled with a pair of scissors for jimmy and centrebit and stole the consul's trousers. But all the telling in print will never make you understand the exquisite finish of a tenement that you could kick in with your foot and pound to match-wood with your fists. Behold a *bunnia*'s shop. He sells rice and chillies and dried fish and wooden scoops made of bamboo. The front of his shop is very solid. It is made of half-inch battens nailed side by side. Not one of the battens is broken; and each one is foursquare perfectly. Feeling ashamed of himself for this surly barring up of his house, he fills one-half the frontage with oiled paper stretched upon quarter-inch framing. Not a single square of oil paper has a hole in it, and not one of the squares, which in more uncivilised countries would hold a pane of glass if strong enough, is out of line. And the *bunnia*, clothed in a blue dressing-gown, with thick white stockings on his feet, sits behind, not among his wares, on a pale gold-coloured mat of soft rice straw bound with black list at the edges. This mat is two inches thick, three feet wide and six long. You might, if you were a sufficient pig, eat your dinner off any portion of it. The *bunnia* lies with one wadded blue arm round a big brazier of hammered brass on which is faintly delineated in incised lines a very terrible dragon. The brazier is full of charcoal ash, but there is no ash on the mat. By the *bunnia*'s side is a pouch of green leather tied with a red silk cord, holding tobacco cut fine as cotton. He fills a long black and red lacquered pipe, lights it at the charcoal in the brazier, takes two whiffs, and the pipe is empty. Still there is no speck on the mat. Behind the *bunnia* is a shadow-screen of bead and bamboo. This veils a room floored with pale gold and roofed with panels of grained cedar. There is nothing in the room save a blood-red blanket laid out smoothly as a sheet of paper. Beyond the room is a passage of polished wood, so polished that it gives back the reflections of the white paper wall. At the end of the passage and clearly visible to this unique *bunnia* is a dwarfed pine two feet high in a green glazed pot, and by its side is a branch of azalea, blood red as the blanket, set in a pale grey crackle-pot. The *bunnia* has put it there for his own pleasure, for the delight of his eyes, because he loves it. The white man has nothing whatever to do with his tastes, and he keeps his house specklessly pure because he likes cleanliness and knows it is artistic. What shall we say to such a *bunnia*?

His brother in Northern India may live behind a front of time-blackened open-work wood, but... I do not think he would grow anything save *tulsi* in a pot, and that only to please the Gods and his womenfolk.

Let us not compare the two men, but go on through Nagasaki.

Except for the horrible policemen who insist on being continental, the people – the common people, that is – do not run after unseemly costumes of the West. The young men wear round felt hats, occasionally coats and trousers, and semi-occasionally boots. All these are vile. In the more metropolitan towns men say Western dress is rather the rule than the exception. If this be so, I am disposed to conclude that the sins of their forefathers in making enterprising Jesuit missionaries into beefsteak have been visited on the Japanese in the shape of a partial obscuration of their artistic instincts. Yet the punishment seems rather too heavy for the offence.

Then I fell admiring the bloom on the people's cheeks, the three-cornered smiles of the fat babes, and the surpassing 'otherness' of everything round me. It is so strange to be in a clean land, and stranger to walk among doll's houses. Japan is a soothing place for a small man. Nobody comes to tower over him, and he looks down upon all the women, as is right and proper. A dealer in curiosities bent himself double on his own doormat, and I passed in, feeling for the first time that I was a barbarian, and no true Sahib. The slush of the streets was thick on my boots, and he, the immaculate owner, asked me to walk across a polished floor and white mats to an inner chamber. He brought me a foot-mat, which only made matters worse, for a pretty girl giggled round the corner as I toiled at it. Japanese shopkeepers ought not to be so clean. I went into a boarded passage about two feet wide, found a gem of a garden of dwarfed trees, in the space of half a tennis court, whacked my head on a fragile lintel, and arrived at a four-walled daintiness where I involuntarily lowered my voice. Do you recollect Mrs Molesworth's *Cuckoo Clock*, and the big cabinet that Griselda entered with the cuckoo? I was not Griselda, but my low-voiced friend, in his long, soft wraps, was the cuckoo, and the room was the cabinet. Again I tried to console myself with the thought that I could kick the place to pieces; but this only made me feel large and coarse and dirty – a most unfavourable mood for bargaining. The cuckoo-man caused pale tea to be brought – just such tea as you read of in books of travel – and the tea completed my embarrassment. What I wanted to say was, 'Look here, you person. You're much too clean and refined for this life here below, and your house is unfit for a man to live in until he has been taught a lot of things which I have never learned. Consequently I hate you because I feel myself your inferior, and you despise me and my boots because you know me for a savage. Let me go, or I'll pull your house of cedar-wood over your ears.' What I really said was, 'Oh, ah yes. Awf'ly pretty. Awful queer way of doing business.'

The cuckoo-man proved to be a horrid extortioner; but I was hot and uncomfortable till I got outside, and was a bog-trotting Briton once more. You have never blundered into the inside of a three-hundred-dollar cabinet, therefore you will not understand me.

We came to the foot of a hill, as it might have been the hill on which the Shway Dagon stands, and up that hill ran a mighty flight of grey, weather-darkened steps, spanned here and there by monolithic *torii*. Everyone knows what a *torii* is. They have them in Southern India. A great King makes a note of the place where he intends to build a huge arch, but being a King does so in stone, not ink – sketches in the air two beams and a cross-bar, forty or sixty feet high, and twenty or thirty wide. In Southern India the cross-bar is humped in the middle. In the Further East it flares up at the ends. This description is hardly according to the books, but if a man begins by consulting books in a new country he is lost. Over the steps hung heavy blue-green or green-black pines, old, gnarled, and bossed. The foliage of the hillside was a lighter green, but the pines set the keynote of colour, and the blue dresses of the few folk on the steps answered it. There was no sunshine in the air, but I vow that sunshine would have spoilt all. We climb for five minutes, I and the Professor and the camera, and then we turned, and saw the roofs of Nagasaki lying at our feet – a sea of lead and dull-brown, with here and there a smudge of creamy pink to mark the bloom of the cherry trees. The hills round the town were speckled with the resting-places of the dead, with clumps of pine and feathery bamboo.

'What a country!' said the Professor, unstrapping his camera. 'And have you noticed, wherever we go there's always some man who knows how to carry my kit? The *gharri* driver at Moulmein handed me my stops; the fellow at Penang knew all about it, too; and the rickshaw coolie has seen a camera before. Curious, isn't it?'

'Professor,' said I, 'it's due to the extraordinary fact that we are not the only people in the world. I began to realise it at Hong Kong. It's getting plainer now. I shouldn't be surprised if we turned out to be ordinary human beings, after all.'

We entered a courtyard where an evil-looking bronze horse stared at two stone lions, and a company of children babbled among themselves. There is a legend connected with the bronze horse, which may be found in the guidebooks. But the real true story of the creature is that he was made long ago out of the fossil ivory of Siberia by a Japanese Prometheus, and got life and many foals, whose descendants closely resemble their father. Long years have almost eliminated the ivory in the blood, but it crops out in creamy mane and tail; and the pot-belly and marvellous feet of the bronze horse may be found to this day among the pack-ponies of Nagasaki, who carry pack-saddles adorned with velvet and red cloth, who wear grass shoes on their hind feet, and who are made like to horses in a pantomime.

We could not go beyond this courtyard because a label said, 'No admittance', and thus all we saw of the temple was rich-brown high roofs of blackened thatch, breaking back and back in wave and undulation till they were lost in the foliage. The Japanese can play with thatch as men play with modelling clay, but how their light underpinnings can carry the weight of the roof is a mystery to the lay eye.

We went down the steps to tiffin, and a half-formed resolve was shaping itself in my heart the while. Burma was a very nice place, but they eat *gnapi* there, and there were smells, and after all, the girls weren't so pretty as some others –

'You must take off your boots,' said Y-Tokai.

I assure you there is no dignity in sitting down on the steps of a teahouse and struggling with muddy boots. And it is impossible to be polite in your stockinged feet when the floor under you is as smooth as glass and a pretty girl wants to know where you would like tiffin. Take at least one pair of beautiful socks with you when you come this way. Get them made of embroidered *sambhur* skin, of silk if you like; but do not stand as I did in cheap striped brown things with a darn at the heel, and try to talk to a tea-girl.

They led us – three of them and all fresh and pretty – into a room furnished with a golden-brown bearskin. The *tokonoma*, recess aforementioned, held one scroll-picture of bats wheeling in the twilight, a bamboo flower-holder, and yellow flowers. The ceiling was of panelled wood, with the exception of one strip at the side nearest the window, and this was made of plaited shavings of cedar-wood, marked off from the rest of the ceiling by a wine-brown bamboo so polished that it might have been lacquered. A touch of the hand sent one side of the room flying back, and we entered a really large room with another *tokonoma* framed on one side by eight or ten feet of an unknown wood, bearing the same grain as a Penang lawyer, and above by a stick of unbarked tree set there purely because it was curiously mottled. In this second *tokonoma* was a pearl-grey vase, and that was all. Two sides of the room were of oiled paper, and the joints of the beams were covered by the brazen images of crabs, half life-size. Save for the sill of the *tokonoma*, which was black lacquer, every inch of wood in the place was natural grain without flaw. Outside was the garden, fringed with a hedge of dwarf-pines and adorned with a tiny pond, water-smoothed stones sunk in the soil, and a blossoming cherry tree.

They left us alone in this paradise of cleanliness and beauty, and being only a shameless Englishman without his boots – a white man is always degraded when he goes barefoot – I wandered round the wall, trying all the screens. It was only when I stooped to examine the sunk catch of a screen that I saw it was a plaque of inlay work representing two white cranes feeding on fish. The whole was about three inches square and in the ordinary course of events would never be looked at. The screens hid a cupboard in which all the lamps and candlesticks and pillows and sleeping-bags of the household seemed to be stored. An Oriental nation that can fill a cupboard tidily is a nation to bow down to. Upstairs I went by a staircase of grained wood and lacquer, into rooms of rarest device with circular windows that opened on nothing, and so were filled with bamboo tracery for the delight of the eye. The passages floored with dark wood shone like ice, and I was ashamed.

'Professor,' said I, 'they don't spit; they don't eat like pigs; they can't quarrel, and a drunken man would reel straight through every portion in the house and roll down the hill into Nagasaki. They can't have any children.' Here I stopped. Downstairs was full of babies.

The maidens came in with tea in blue china and cake in a red lacquered bowl – such cake as one gets at one or two houses in Simla. We sprawled ungracefully on red rugs over the mats, and they gave us chopsticks to separate the cake with. It was a long task.

'Is that all?' growled the Professor. 'I'm hungry, and cake and tea oughtn't to come till four o'clock.' Here he took a wedge of cake furtively with his hands.

They returned – five of them this time – with black lacquer stands a foot square and four inches high. Those were our tables. They bore a red lacquered bowlful of fish boiled in brine, and sea-anemones. At least they were not mushrooms. A paper napkin tied with gold thread enclosed our chopsticks; and in a little flat saucer lay a smoked crayfish, a slice of a compromise that looked like Yorkshire pudding and tasted like sweet omelette, and a twisted fragment of some translucent thing that had once been alive but was now pickled. They went away, but not empty handed, for thou, oh, O-Toyo, didst take away my heart – same which I gave to the Burmese girl in the Shway Dagon pagoda!

The Professor opened his eyes a little, but said no word. The chopsticks demanded all his attention, and the return of the girls took up the rest. O-Toyo, ebon-haired, rosy-cheeked, and made throughout of delicate porcelain, laughed at me because I devoured all the mustard sauce that had been served with my raw fish, and wept copiously till she gave me *saki* from a lordly bottle about four inches high. If you took some very thin hock, and tried to mull it and forgot all about the brew till it was half cold, you would get *saki*. I had mine in a saucer so tiny that I was bold to have it filled eight or ten times and loved O-Toyo none the less at the end.

After raw fish and mustard sauce came some other sort of fish cooked with pickled radishes, and very slippery on the chopsticks. The girls knelt in a semicircle and shrieked with delight at the Professor's clumsiness, for indeed it was not I that nearly upset the dinner table in a vain attempt to recline gracefully. After the bamboo-shoots came a basin of white beans in sweet sauce – very tasty indeed. Try to convey beans to your mouth with a pair of wooden knitting-needles and see what happens. Some chicken cunningly boiled with turnips, and a bowlful of snow-white boneless fish and a pile of rice, concluded the meal. I have forgotten one or two of the courses, but when O-Toyo handed me the tiny lacquered Japanese pipe full of hay-like tobacco, I counted nine dishes in the lacquer stand – each dish representing a course. Then O-Toyo and I smoked by alternate pipefuls.

My very respectable friends at all the clubs and messes, have you ever after a good tiffin lolled on cushions and smoked, with one pretty girl to fill your pipe and four to admire you in an unknown tongue? You do not know what life is. I looked round me at that faultless room, at the dwarf pines and creamy cherry blossoms without, at O-Toyo bubbling with laughter because I blew smoke through my nose, and at the ring of *Mikado* maidens over against the golden-brown bearskin rug. Here was colour, form, food, comfort, and beauty enough for half a year's contemplation. I would not be a Burman any more. I would be a Japanese – always with O-Toyo – in a cabinet workhouse on a camphor-scented hillside.

'Heigh-ho!' said the Professor. 'There are worse places than this to live and die in. D'you know our steamer goes at four? Let's ask for the bill and get away.'

Now I have left my heart with O-Toyo under the pines. Perhaps I shall get it back at Kobé.

Explains in what manner I was taken to Venice in the rain, and climbed into a devil fort; a tin-pot exhibition, and a bath. Of the maiden and the boltless door, the cultivator and his fields, and the manufacture of ethnological theories at railroad speed. Ends with Kyoto.

'Come along to Osaka,' said the Professor.

'Why? I'm quite comfy here, and we shall have lobster cutlets for tiffin; and, anyhow, it is raining heavily, and we shall get wet.'

Sorely against my will – for it was in my mind to fudge Japan from a guidebook while I enjoyed the cookery of the Oriental at Kobé – I was dragged into a rickshaw and the rain, and conveyed to a railway station. Even the Japanese cannot make their railway stations lovely, though they do their best. Their system of baggage-booking is borrowed from the Americans; their narrow-gauge lines, locos, and rolling stock are English; their passenger-traffic is regulated with the precision of the Gaul, and the uniforms of their officials come from the nearest ragbag. The passengers themselves were altogether delightful. A large number of them were modified Europeans, and resembled nothing more than Tenniel's picture of the White Rabbit on the first page of *Alice in Wonderland*. They were dressed in neat little tweed suits with fawn-coloured overcoats, and they carried ladies' reticules of black leather and nickel platings. They wore paper and celluloid stuck-up collars which must have been quite thirteen inches round the neck, and their boots were number fours. On their hands – their wee, wee hands – they had white cotton gloves, and they smoked cigarettes from fairy little cigarette cases. That was young Japan – the Japan of the present day.

'Wah, wah, God is great,' said the Professor. 'But it isn't in human nature for a man who sprawls about on soft mats by instinct to wear Europe clothes as though they belonged to him. If you notice, the last thing that they take to is shoes.'

A lapis-lazuli coloured locomotive which, by accident, had a mixed train attached to it happened to loaf up to the platform just then, and we entered a first-class English compartment. There was no stupid double roof, window shade, or abortive thermantidote. It was a London and South-Western carriage. Osaka is about eighteen miles from Kobé, and stands at the head of the bay of Osaka. The train is allowed to go as fast as fifteen miles an hour and to play at the stations all along the line. You must know that the line runs between the hills and the shore, and the drainage-fall is a great deal steeper than anything we have between Saharunpur and Umballa. The rivers and the hill torrents come down straight from the hills on raised beds of their own formation, which beds again have to be bunded and spanned with girder bridges or – here, perhaps, I may be wrong – tunnelled.

The stations are black-tiled, red-walled, and concrete-floored, and all the plant from signal levers to goods-truck is English. The official colour of the bridges is a yellow-brown most like unto a faded chrysanthemum. The uniform of the ticket-collectors is a peaked forage cap with gold lines, black frock-coat with brass buttons, very long in the skirt, trousers with black mohair braid, and buttoned kid boots. You cannot be rude to a man in such raiment.

But the countryside was the thing that made us open our eyes. Imagine a land of rich black soil, very heavily manured, and worked by the spade and hoe almost exclusively, and if you split your field (of vision) into half-acre plots, you will get a notion of the raw material the cultivator works on. But all I can write will give you no notion of the wantonness of neatness visible in the fields, of the elaborate system of irrigation, and the mathematical precision of the planting. There was no mixing of crops, no waste of boundary in footpath, and no difference of value in the land. The water stood everywhere within ten feet of the surface, as the well-sweeps attested. On the slopes of the foot-hills each drop between the levels was neatly riveted with unmortared stones, and the edges of the watercuts were faced in like manner. The young rice was transplanted very much as draughts are laid on the board; the tea might have been cropped garden box; and between the lines of the mustard the water lay in the drills as in a wooden trough, while the purple of the beans ran up to the mustard and stopped as though cut with a rule.

On the seaboard we saw an almost continuous line of towns variegated with factory chimneys; inland, the crazy-quilt of green, dark-green and gold. Even in the rain the view was lovely, and exactly as Japanese pictures had led me to hope for. Only one drawback occurred to the Professor and myself at the same time. Crops don't grow to the full limit of the seed on heavily worked ground dotted with villages except at a price.

'Cholera?' said I, watching a stretch of well-sweeps.

'Cholera,' said the Professor. 'Must be, y'know. It's all sewage irrigation.'

I felt that I was friends with the cultivators at once. These broad-hatted, blue-clad gentlemen who tilled their fields by hand – except when they borrowed the village buffalo to drive the share through the rice-slough – knew what the scourge meant.

'How much do you think the Government takes in revenue from vegetable gardens of that kind?' I demanded.

'Bosh,' said he, quietly, 'you aren't going to describe the land-tenure of Japan. Look at the yellow of the mustard!'

It lay in sheets round the line. It ran up the hills to the dark pines. It rioted over the brown sandbars of the swollen rivers, and faded away by mile after mile to the shores of the leaden sea. The high-peaked houses of brown thatch stood knee-deep in it, and it surged up to the factory chimneys of Osaka.

'Great place, Osaka,' said the guide. 'All sorts of manufactures there.'

Osaka is built into and over and among 1894 canals, rivers, dams, and watercuts. What the multitudinous chimneys mean I cannot tell. They have something to do with rice and cotton; but it is not good that the Japanese should indulge in trade, and I will not call Osaka a 'great commercial *entrepot*'. 'People who live in paper houses should never sell goods,' as the proverb says.

Because of his many wants there is but one hotel for the Englishman in Osaka, and they call it Juter's. Here the views of two civilisations collide and the result is awful. The building is altogether Japanese; wood and tile and sliding screen from top to bottom; but the fitments are mixed. My room, for instance, held a *tokonoma*, made of the polished black stem of a palm and delicate woodwork, framing a scroll picture representing storks. But on the floor over the white mats lay a Brussels carpet that made the indignant toes tingle. From the back veranda one overhung the river which ran straight as an arrow between two lines of houses. They have cabinet-makers in Japan to fit the rivers to the towns. From my veranda I could see three bridges – one a hideous lattice-girder arrangement – and part of a fourth. We were on an island and owned a water-gate if we wanted to take a boat.

Apropos of water, be pleased to listen to a Shocking Story. It is written in all the books that the Japanese though cleanly are somewhat casual in their customs. They bathe often with nothing on and together. This notion my experience of the country, gathered in the seclusion of the Oriental at Kobé, made me scoff at. I demanded a tub at Juter's. The infinitesimal man led me down verandas and upstairs to a beautiful bath-house full of hot and cold water and fitted with cabinet-work, somewhere in a lonely out-gallery. There was naturally no bolt to the door any more than there would be a bolt to a dining room. Had I been sheltered by the walls of a big Europe bath, I should not have cared, but I was preparing to wash when a pretty maiden opened the door, and indicated that she also would tub in the deep, sunken Japanese bath at my side. When one is dressed only in one's virtue and a pair of spectacles it is difficult to shut the door in the face of a girl. She gathered that I was not happy, and withdrew giggling, while I thanked heaven, blushing profusely the while, that I had been brought up in a society which unfits a man to bathe *à deux*. Even an experience of the Paddington Swimming Baths would have helped me; but coming straight from India Lady Godiva was a ballet-girl in sentiment compared to this Actæon.

It rained monsoonishly, and the Professor discovered a castle which he needs must see. 'It's Osaka Castle,' he said, 'and it has been fought over for hundreds of years. Come along.'

'I've seen castles in India. Raighur, Jodhpur – all sorts of places. Let's have some more boiled salmon. It's good in this station.'

'Pig,' said the Professor.

We threaded our way over the 4,052 canals, etc., where the little children played with the swiftly running water, and never a mother said 'Don't,' till our rickshaw stopped outside a fort ditch thirty feet deep, and faced with gigantic granite slabs. On the far side uprose the walls of a fort. But such a fort! Fifty feet was the height of the wall, and never a pinch of mortar in the whole. Nor was the face perpendicular, but curved like the ram of a man-of-war. They know the curve in China, and I have seen French artists introduce it into books describing a devil-besieged city of Tartary. Possibly everybody else knows it too, but that is not my affair; life as I have said being altogether new to me. The stone was granite, and the men of old time had used it like mud. The dressed blocks that made the profile of the angles were from twenty feet long, ten or twelve feet high, and as many in thickness. There was no attempt at binding, but there was no fault in the jointing.

'And the little Japs built this!' I cried, awe-stricken at the quarries that rose round me.

'Cyclopean masonry,' grunted the Professor, punching with a stick a monolith of seventeen feet cube. 'Not only did they build it, but they took it. Look at this. Fire!'

The stones had been split and bronzed in places, and the cleavage was the cleavage of fire. Evil must it have been for the armies that led the assault on these monstrous walls. Castles in India I know, and the forts of great Emperors I had seen, but neither Akbar in the north, nor Scindia in the south, had built after this fashion – without ornament, without colour, but with a single eye to savage strength and the utmost purity of line. Perhaps the fort would have looked less forbidding in sunlight. The grey, rain-laden atmosphere through which I saw it suited its spirit. The barracks of the garrison, the commandant's very dainty house, a peach-garden, and two deer were foreign to the place. They should have peopled it with giants from the mountains, instead of – Gurkhas! A Japanese infantryman is not a Gurkha, though he might be mistaken for one as long as he stood still. The sentry at the quarter-guard belonged, I fancy, to the 4th Regiment. His uniform was black or blue, with red facings, and shoulder-straps carrying the number of the regiment in cloth. The rain necessitated an overcoat, but why he should have carried knapsack, blanket, boots, *and* binoculars I could not fathom. The knapsack was of cowskin with the hair on, the boots were strapped soles, cut on each side, while a heavy country blanket was rolled U-shape over the head of the knapsack, fitting close to the back. In the place usually occupied by the mess-tin was a black leather case shaped like a field-glass. This must be a mistake of mine, but I can only record as I see. The rifle was a side-bolt weapon of some kind, and the bayonet an uncommonly good sword one, locked to the muzzle, English fashion. The ammunition pouches, as far as I could see under the greatcoat, ran on the belt in front, and were double-strapped down. White spatterdashes – very dirty – and peaked cap completed the outfit. I surveyed the man with interest, and would have made further examination of him but for fear of the big bayonet. His arms were well kept – not speckless by any means – but his uniform would have made an English colonel swear. There was no portion of his body except the neck that it pretended to fit. I peeped into the quarter-guard. Fans and dainty tea-sets do not go with one's notions of a barrack. One drunken defaulter of certain far away regiments that I could name would not only have cleared out that quarter-guard, but brought away all its fittings except the rifle-racks. Yet the little men, who were always gentle, and never got drunk, were mounting guard over a pile that, with a blue fire on the bastions, might have served for the guard-gates of Hell.

I climbed to the top of the fort and was rewarded by a view of thirty miles of country, chiefly pale yellow mustard and blue-green pine, and the sight of the very large city of Osaka fading away into mist. The guide took most pleasure in the factory chimneys. 'There is an exposition here – an exposition of industrialities. Come and see,' said he. He took us down from that high place and showed us the glory of the land in the shape of corkscrews, tin mugs, egg-whisks, dippers, silks, buttons, and all the trumpery that can be stitched on a card and sold for five-pence three farthings. The Japanese unfortunately make all these things for themselves, and are proud of it. They have nothing to learn from the West as far as finish is concerned, and by intuition know how to case and mount wares tastefully. The exposition was in four large sheds running round a central building which held only screens, pottery, and cabinet-ware loaned for the occasion. I rejoiced to see that the common people did not care for the penknives, and the pencils, and the mock jewellery. They left those sheds alone and discussed the screens, first taking off their clogs that the inlaid floor of the room might not suffer. Of all the gracious things I beheld, two only remain in my memory – one a screen in grey representing the heads of six devils instinct with malice and hate; the other, a bold sketch in monochrome of an old woodcutter wrestling with the down-bent branch of a tree. Two hundred years have passed since the artist dropped his pencil, but you may almost hear the tough wood jar under the stroke of the chopper, as the old man puts his back into the task and draws in the labouring breath. There is a picture by Legros of a beggar dying in a ditch, which might have been suggested by that screen.

Next morning, after a night's rain, which sent the river racing under the frail balconies at eight miles an hour, the sun broke through the clouds. Is this a little matter to you who can count upon him daily? I had not seen him since March, and was beginning to feel anxious. Then the land of peach blossom spread its draggled wings abroad and rejoiced. All the pretty maidens put on their loveliest crêpe sashes – fawn colour, pink, blue, orange, and lilac – all the little children picked up a baby each, and went out to be happy. In a temple garden full of blossom I performed the miracle of Deucalion with two cents' worth of sweets. The babies swarmed on the instant, till, for fear of raising all the mothers too, I forbore to give them any more. They smiled and nodded prettily, and trotted after me, forty strong, the big ones helping the little, and the little ones skipping in the puddles. A Japanese child never cries, never scuffles, never fights, and never makes mud pies except when it lives on the banks of a canal. Yet, lest it should spread its sash-bow and become a bald-headed angel ere its time, Providence has decreed that it should never, never blow its little nose. Notwithstanding the defect, I love it.

There was no business in Osaka that day because of the sunshine and the budding of the trees. Everybody went to a teahouse with his friends. I went also, but first ran along a boulevard by the side of the river, pretending to look at the mint. This was only a common place of solid granite where they turn out dollars and rubbish of that kind. All along the boulevard the cherry, peach, and plum trees, pink, white, and red, touched branches and made a belt of velvety soft colour as far as the eye could reach. Weeping willows were the normal ornaments of the waterside, this revel of bloom being only part of the prodigality of Spring. The Mint may make a hundred thousand dollars a day, but all the silver in its keeping will not bring again the three weeks of the peach blossom which, even beyond the chrysanthemum, is the crown and glory of Japan. For some act of surpassing merit performed in a past life I have been enabled to hit those three weeks in the middle.

'Now is the Japanese festival of the cherry blossom,' said the guide. 'All the people will be festive. They will pray too and go to the tea-gardens.'

Now you might wall an Englishman about with cherry trees in bloom from head to heel, and after the first day he would begin to complain of the smell. As you know, the Japanese arrange a good many of their festivals in honour of flowers, and this is surely commendable, for blossoms are the most tolerant of gods.

The teahouse system of the Japanese filled me with pleasure at a pleasure that I could not fully comprehend. It pays a company in Osaka to build on the outskirts of the town a nine-storied pagoda of wood and iron, to lay out elaborate gardens round it, and to hang the whole with strings of blood-red lanterns, because the Japanese will come wherever there is a good view to sit on a mat and discuss tea and sweetmeats and *saki*. This Eiffel Tower is, to tell the truth, anything but pretty, yet the surroundings redeem it. Although it was not quite completed, the lower storeys were full of tea-stalls and tea-drinkers. The men and women were obviously admiring the view. It is an astounding thing to see an Oriental so engaged; it is as though he had stolen something from a sahib.

From Osaka – canal-cut, muddy, and fascinating Osaka – the Professor, Mister Yamagutchi – the guide – and I took train to Kyoto, an hour from Osaka. On the road I saw four buffaloes at as many rice-ploughs – which was noticeable as well as wasteful. A buffalo at rest must cover the half of a Japanese field; but perhaps they are kept on the mountain ledges and only pulled down when wanted. The Professor says that what I call buffalo is really bullock. The worst of travelling with an accurate man is his accuracy. We argued about the Japanese in the train, about his present and his future, and the manner in which he has ranged himself on the side of the grosser nations of the earth.

'Did it hurt his feelings very much to wear our clothes? Didn't he rebel when he put on a pair of trousers for the first time? Won't he grow sensible some day and drop foreign habits?' These were some of the questions I put to the landscape and the Professor.

'He was a baby,' said the latter, 'a big baby. I think his sense of humour was at the bottom of the change, but he didn't know that a nation which once wears trousers never takes 'em off. You see "enlightened" Japan is only one-and-twenty years old, and people are not very wise at one-and-twenty. Read Reed's *Japan* and learn how the change came about. There was a Mikado and a *Shogun* who was Sir Frederick Roberts, but he tried to be the Viceroy and –'

'Bother the *Shogun*! I've seen something like the Babu class, and something like the farmer class. What I want to see is the Rajput class – the man who used to wear the thousands and thousands of swords in the curio-shops. Those swords were as much made for use as a Rajputana sabre. Where are the men who used 'em? Show me a Samurai.'

The Professor answered not a word, but scrutinised heads on the wayside platforms. 'I take it that the high-arched forehead, club nose, and eyes close together – the Spanish type – are from Rajput stock, while the German-faced Japanese is the Khattri – the lower class.'

Thus we talked of the natures and dispositions of men we knew nothing about till we had decided (1) that the painful politeness of the Japanese nation rose from the habit, dropped only twenty years ago, of extended and emphatic sword-wearing, even as the Rajput is the pink of courtesy because his friend goes armed; (2) that this politeness will disappear in another generation, or will at least be seriously impaired; (3) that the cultured Japanese man of the English pattern will corrupt and defile the tastes of his neighbours till (4) Japan altogether ceases to exist as a separate nation and becomes a button-hook manufacturing appanage of America; (5) that these things being so, and sure to happen in two or three hundred years, the Professor and I were lucky to reach Japan betimes; and (6) that it was foolish to form theories about the country until we had seen a little of it.

So we came to the city of Kyoto in regal sunshine, tempered by a breeze that drove the cherry blossoms in drifts about the streets. One Japanese town, in the southern provinces at least, is very like another to look at – a grey-black sea of house roofs, speckled with the white walls of the fire-proof godowns where merchants and rich men keep their chief treasures. The general level is broken by the temple roofs, which are turned up at the edges, and remotely resemble so many terai-hats. Kyoto fills a plain almost entirely surrounded by wooded hills, very familiar in their aspect to those who have seen the Siwaliks. Once upon a time it was the capital of Japan, and today numbers 250,000 people. It is laid out like an American town. All the streets run at right angles to each other. That, by the way, is exactly what the Professor and I are doing. We are elaborating the theory of the Japanese people, and we can't agree.

Biographical note

Born in Bombay, India in 1865, Joseph Rudyard Kipling was the son of John Lockwood Kipling, an artist and a teacher, and his wife Alice. At the age of five, he was sent to England to stay with a foster family at Southsea in Hampshire, and at twelve was sent to be educated at the United Services College at Westward Ho! in Devon.

He returned to India at sixteen, where he began a career in journalism, sub-editing the *Civil and Military Gazette* in Lahore before being promoted to *The Pioneer* in Allahabad in 1887. During this time, he wrote the stories that would eventually appear in *Plain Tales from the Hills* (1888), *Soldiers Three* (1888) and *Wee Willie Winkie* (1888).

In 1889, Kipling returned to London where he won success with the novel *The Light that Failed* (1890) and *Barrack-room Ballads* (1892). In 1892, he married and embarked on a world trip, before settling in Vermont where his first two children were born. It was here he produced the two *Jungle Books* (1894 and 1895) and *Captains Courageous* (1897).

Kipling returned to England in 1896, moving to Rottingdean in Sussex where his son was born and where he wrote the picaresque novel *Kim* (1901) and the *Just So Stories* (1902). Tragically, his elder daughter died in 1899 and in 1902 Kipling and his family sought the seclusion of 'Bateman's', a house near Burwash in Sussex, where he wrote *Puck of Pook's Hill* (1906) and *Rewards and Fairies* (1910), which included the poem 'If–'.

Kipling was awarded the Nobel Prize for Literature in 1907. He died in 1936 aged seventy and is buried at Poet's Corner in Westminster Abbey.

Under our three imprints, Hesperus Press publishes over 300 books by many of the greatest figures in worldwide literary history, as well as contemporary and debut authors well worth discovering.

Hesperus Classics handpicks the best of worldwide and translated literature, introducing forgotten and neglected books to new generations.

Hesperus Nova showcases quality contemporary fiction and non-fiction designed to entertain and inspire.

Hesperus Minor rediscovers well-loved children's books from the past – these are books which will bring back fond memories for adults, which they will want to share with their children and loved ones.

To find out more visit www.hesperuspress.com
@HesperusPress

SELECTED TITLES FROM HESPERUS PRESS

Author	Title	Foreword writer
Pietro Aretino	*The School of Whoredom*	Paul Bailey
Pietro Aretino	*The Secret Life of Nuns*	
Jane Austen	*Lesley Castle*	Zoë Heller
Jane Austen	*Love and Friendship*	Fay Weldon
Honoré de Balzac	*Colonel Chabert*	A.N. Wilson
Charles Baudelaire	*On Wine and Hashish*	Margaret Drabble
Giovanni Boccaccio	*Life of Dante*	A.N. Wilson
Charlotte Brontë	*The Spell*	
Emily Brontë	*Poems of Solitude*	Helen Dunmore
Mikhail Bulgakov	*Fatal Eggs*	Doris Lessing
Mikhail Bulgakov	*The Heart of a Dog*	A.S. Byatt
Giacomo Casanova	*The Duel*	Tim Parks
Miguel de Cervantes	*The Dialogue of the Dogs*	Ben Okri
Geoffrey Chaucer	*The Parliament of Birds*	
Anton Chekhov	*The Story of a Nobody*	Louis de Bernières
Anton Chekhov	*Three Years*	William Fiennes
Wilkie Collins	*The Frozen Deep*	
Joseph Conrad	*Heart of Darkness*	A.N. Wilson
Joseph Conrad	*The Return*	Colm Tóibín
Gabriele D'Annunzio	*The Book of the Virgins*	Tim Parks
Dante Alighieri	*The Divine Comedy: Inferno*	
Dante Alighieri	*New Life*	Louis de Bernières
Daniel Defoe	*The King of Pirates*	Peter Ackroyd
Marquis de Sade	*Incest*	Janet Street-Porter
Charles Dickens	*The Haunted House*	Peter Ackroyd
Charles Dickens	*A House to Let*	
Fyodor Dostoevsky	The Double	Jeremy Dyson
Fyodor Dostoevsky	Poor People	Charlotte Hobson
Alexandre Dumas	*One Thousand and One Ghosts*	

Author	Title	Contributor
George Eliot	*Amos Barton*	Matthew Sweet
Henry Fielding	*Jonathan Wild the Great*	Peter Ackroyd
F. Scott Fitzgerald	*The Popular Girl*	Helen Dunmore
Gustave Flaubert	Memoirs of a Madman	Germaine Greer
Ugo Foscolo	*Last Letters of Jacopo Ortis*	Valerio Massimo Manfredi
Elizabeth Gaskell	*Lois the Witch*	Jenny Uglow
Théophile Gautier	*The Jinx*	Gilbert Adair
André Gide	*Theseus*	
Johann Wolfgang von Goethe	*The Man of Fifty*	A.S. Byatt
Nikolai Gogol	*The Squabble*	Patrick McCabe
E.T.A. Hoffmann	*Mademoiselle de Scudéri*	Gilbert Adair
Victor Hugo	*The Last Day of a Condemned Man*	Libby Purves
Joris-Karl Huysmans	*With the Flow*	Simon Callow
Henry James	*In the Cage*	Libby Purves
Franz Kafka	*Metamorphosis*	Martin Jarvis
Franz Kafka	*The Trial*	Zadie Smith
John Keats	*Fugitive Poems*	Andrew Motion
Heinrich von Kleist	*The Marquise of O–*	Andrew Miller
Mikhail Lermontov	*A Hero of Our Time*	Doris Lessing
Nikolai Leskov	*Lady Macbeth of Mtsensk*	Gilbert Adair
Carlo Levi	*Words are Stones*	Anita Desai
Xavier de Maistre	*A Journey Around my Room*	Alain de Botton
André Malraux	*The Way of the Kings*	Rachel Seiffert
Katherine Mansfield	*Prelude*	William Boyd
Edgar Lee Masters	*Spoon River Anthology*	Shena Mackay
Guy de Maupassant	*Butterball*	Germaine Greer
Prosper Mérimée	*Carmen*	Philip Pullman
Sir Thomas More	*The History of King Richard III*	Sister Wendy Beckett
Sándor Petőfi	*John the Valiant*	George Szirtes
Francis Petrarch	*My Secret Book*	Germaine Greer

Luigi Pirandello	*Loveless Love*	
Edgar Allan Poe	*Eureka*	Sir Patrick Moore
Alexander Pope	*The Rape of the Lock and A Key to the Lock*	Peter Ackroyd
Antoine-François Prévost	*Manon Lescaut*	Germaine Greer
Marcel Proust	*Pleasures and Days*	A.N. Wilson
Alexander Pushkin	*Dubrovsky*	Patrick Neate
Alexander Pushkin	*Ruslan and Lyudmila*	Colm Tóibín
François Rabelais	*Pantagruel*	Paul Bailey
François Rabelais	*Gargantua*	Paul Bailey
Christina Rossetti	*Commonplace*	Andrew Motion
George Sand	*The Devil's Pool*	Victoria Glendinning
Jean-Paul Sartre	*The Wall*	Justin Cartwright
Friedrich von Schiller	*The Ghost-seer*	Martin Jarvis
Mary Shelley	*Transformation*	
Percy Bysshe Shelley	*Zastrozzi*	Germaine Greer
Stendhal	*Memoirs of an Egotist*	Doris Lessing
Robert Louis Stevenson	*Dr Jekyll and Mr Hyde*	Helen Dunmore
Theodor Storm	*The Lake of the Bees*	Alan Sillitoe
Leo Tolstoy	*The Death of Ivan Ilych*	
Leo Tolstoy	*Hadji Murat*	Colm Tóibín
Ivan Turgenev	*Faust*	Simon Callow
Mark Twain	*The Diary of Adam and Eve*	John Updike
Mark Twain	*Tom Sawyer, Detective*	
Oscar Wilde	*The Portrait of Mr W.H.*	Peter Ackroyd
Virginia Woolf	*Carlyle's House and Other Sketches*	Doris Lessing
Virginia Woolf	*Monday or Tuesday*	Scarlett Thomas
Emile Zola	*For a Night of Love*	A.N. Wilson

OTHER TITLES IN THE HESPERUS ON SERIES

Author	Title	Foreword writer
Charles Baudelaire	*On wine and hashish*	Margaret Drabble
Robert Burton	*On melancholy*	
G.K. Chesterton	*On tremendous trifles*	Ben Schott
Arthur Conan Doyle	*On the unexplained*	
Charles Dickens	*On London*	
Charles Dickens	*On poverty*	
Charles Dickens	*On theatre*	
Charles Dickens	*On travel*	
John Donne	*On death*	Edward Docx
Sigmund Freud	*On cocaine*	
William Hazlitt	*On the elgin marbles*	Tom Paulin
Ernest Hemingway	*On Paris*	
Harry Houdini	*On deception*	Derren Brown
Henry James	*On Provence*	
Jerome K. Jerome	*On the art of making up one's mind*	Joseph Connolly
John Stuart Mill	*On the subjection of women*	Fay Weldon
Marcel Proust	*On reading*	Eric Karpeles
John Ruskin		
Joseph Roth	*On the end of the world*	
John Ruskin	*On genius and the common man*	Melvyn Bragg
Bernard Shaw	*On war*	Philip Pullman
Stendhal	*On love*	A.C. Grayling
Mark Twain	*On Europe*	
Virginia Woolf	*On fiction*	
Virginia Woolf	*On not knowing Greek*	